EFFECTIVE IN-CLASS SUPPORT

The Management of Support Staff in
Mainstream and Special Schools

Stephanie Lorenz

David Fulton Publishers
London

Dedication

This book is dedicated to my daughter Amy, who displays all the qualities of a natural team player.

David Fulton Publishers Ltd
Ormond House, 26–27 Boswell Street, London WC1N 3JD

First published in Great Britain by David Fulton Publishers 1998

Note: The right of Stephanie Lorenz to be identified as the author of this work has been asserted by her in accordance with the Copyright, Designs and Patents Act 1988

Copyright © Stephanie Lorenz 1998

British Library Cataloguing in Publication Data
A catalogue record for this book is available from the British Library

ISBN 1-85346-505-4

All rights reserved. No part of this publication may be reproduced, stored in a retrieval system or transmitted, in any form, or by any means, electronic, mechanical, photocopying, recording or otherwise, without the prior permission of the publisher.

Typeset by Textype Typesetters, Cambridge
Printed in Great Britain by Bell and Bain, Glasgow

Contents

	Acknowledgements	v
1	**Introduction**	1
	A history of support	1
	Aims of support	3
	Patterns of employment	7
	Support and training	9
2	**Meeting Children's Needs**	13
	Supporting slow learners	13
	Supporting children with specific learning difficulties	15
	Supporting children with physical difficulties	17
	Supporting children with emotional and behavioural problems	21
3	**Support in the Primary School**	25
	The role of the nursery nurse	25
	Working with classroom assistants	27
	The bilingual language assistant	30
	Parents in the classroom	33
4	**Support at Secondary Level**	39
	The role of the support teacher	39
	Teaching in partnership	42
	Working with support assistants	45
	Developing a support timetable	48
5	**Support in the Special School**	53
	The role of the special school assistant	53
	Therapy in the classroom	56
	Developing multidisciplinary teams	59
	Approaches to room management	61
6	**Putting Support on the Agenda**	65
	Recruitment and selection	65
	Drawing up a job description	68
	Building effective teams	74
	Induction and basic training	77

7 Support Systems for Support Staff	81
Health and safety issues	81
Supervision and appraisal	86
Continuing professional development	90
Supporting the development of inclusive schools	92
References	97
Index	105

Acknowledgements

In preparing this book I have sought help from a large number of friends and colleagues who share my interest in meeting the needs of children with disabilities and in supporting the staff who work with them.

In developing my knowledge of children for whom English is a second language, I am indebted to Daryl Hall who gave her time to overcome my ignorance in this important area, and to Pinoki Ghoshal who kindly allowed me to use some of the materials from the Bury EAL (English as an Additional Language) Service.

In looking at special school issues, I received help and encouragement from Barbara Rossington and the staff at Millwood School. Their head teacher Bernard Emblem generously shared job descriptions and evaluations of staff roles. Support also came from Penny Lacey in Birmingham.

Discussions with Alison Bearn, among others, helped clarify my thinking on issues in the mainstream, while Andy Margerison and Jennifer Martinez enlightened me on the role of the Learning Support Assistant (LSA) and the behaviour support teacher in supporting children with emotional and behavioural problems.

My thinking on the needs of support assistants has been developing over a number of years and has been informed particularly by conversations with Terry Clayton, Richard Parker, Maggie Balshaw, Alan Reynolds, Lynn Turner, David Clarke and Marjorie Sunderland. Lucy Mason kindly allowed me to use the job description she wrote for her new support assistant and Trish Dawson gave me permission to include proformas from Bury.

Margaret Graham, Joyce Berry, Phyllis Ward and Trish Dawson of the Bury Learning Support Service have been particularly helpful and many of the checklists and procedures in the book have been included with their permission. I am also most grateful to Michael Stephenson of CLASS (the Confederation of Learning Assistants with Specialist Skills) and to all the support assistants with whom I have worked. They have helped me see the world from the LSA's viewpoint.

Draft copies of assorted chapters have been read by Pat Birchenough, Alison Bearn, Bernard Emblem and Michael Stephenson who have helped me enormously with their comments. Particular thanks go to Trish Dawson and Margaret Graham, who, despite a looming OFSTED inspection, have found the time to read the final version and provide informed feedback.

Finally, as always, my thanks go to my husband Roger for his forbearance when faced with a wife in manic writing mode.

Chapter 1

Introduction

For the majority of children in most schools, be they primary, secondary or special, the experience of being 'taught' for at least part of the week by more than one adult is a commonplace occurrence.

- Special schools have traditionally employed care staff to attend to the welfare needs of pupils and to work alongside teachers in the classroom.
- Nursery schools and classes are almost invariably staffed by a mixture of teachers and nursery nurses, who work cooperatively to meet the needs of young children.
- In the primary school, the presence of parents and other volunteers hearing children read and supporting them in a range of practical activities is now a regular feature of school life.
- With the help of government funding many second language learners in multiracial schools have benefited from the support of bilingual support staff in the classroom. By 1993, some 14,000 additional teachers and non-teaching staff were being employed by Local Education Authorities (LEAs) to give pupils from the ethnic minorities equality of access to the National Curriculum (OFSTED 1994).
- In the special needs area, Thomas (1990) lists a whole range of people who might be found working alongside the class teacher in a mainstream school:

    (i) special school teachers working in an outreach capacity, sharing their skills with mainstream staff;
    (ii) welfare assistants supporting statemented children;
    (iii) peripatetic teachers co-teaching with mainstream colleagues;
    (iv) secondary remedial teachers offering in-class support to individual students or helping subject staff adapt their approaches to meet the needs of the least able.

During the 1970s and 1980s, there was a significant attitude change within the field of remedial education, crystallised in the

A history of support

recommendations of the Bullock Report (DES 1975) and the Warnock Report (DES 1978). Members of both committees shared the view that remedial or special educational provision in mainstream schools should be more closely related to the child's overall learning experiences. Withdrawal was considered to be a 'bad thing' as it was seen to stigmatise students and result in their receiving a restricted curriculum. Skills acquired in a structured setting were rarely transferred back into the classroom and expectations of remedial students was generally low (Edwards 1985). Thus schools were encouraged to move away from remedial classes and small withdrawal groups towards in-class support.

During the same period there was a parallel development in the use of ancillary staff. As early as 1967, the Plowden Report (DES 1967) identified a group of non-teaching staff in mainstream schools, who had a key role to play in supporting teachers in the classroom. The 'primary school survey' in Scotland (Duthie 1970) indicated appropriate tasks which classroom auxiliaries might undertake, proposed policies for employing them and discussed possible problems. By 1978, the Warnock Report (DES 1978) was noting the presence of support staff carrying out educational programmes as directed by the teacher, as well as providing care for pupils with special educational needs (SEN) in the mainstream.

In the special school sector, the presence of nursery nurses and care assistants, working alongside teachers in the classroom, has been the norm for even longer. The transformation of training centres into special schools for pupils with severe learning difficulties, following the 1970 Education Act (DES 1970) resulted in many former care staff being retained to support children in the classroom. However, there is no doubt that the practice of employing welfare staff was established well before this, for example in schools for pupils with physical disabilities which had existed from the early years of the century.

The recommended ratio of teaching and non-teaching staff to special school pupils with differing levels of need, was laid down by the government in Circular 11/90 (DES 1990), although many LEAs are still failing to achieve these ratios. More recently, with the advent of local management, a number of special school heads have been choosing to increase the ratio of support staff to teachers, thus improving the adult:child ratio without incurring additional costs. Further, as Male (1996b) comments, in some special schools qualified nursery nurses are being replaced by unqualified support assistants.

Although many people (e.g. Marland 1978) have argued that a further increase in the use of auxiliary staff would be a cost-effective way of increasing the productivity of teachers, there has, until quite recently, been more interest in the development of parental involvement schemes than in the use of paid support staff in schools. Nevertheless, the implementation of the 1981 Education Act (DES 1981) led to a rapid increase in the number of ancillary staff being taken on to support the growing population of children with identified special needs in mainstream classes (Goacher *et al.* 1988).

Clayton *et al.* (1989) recorded an increase of 382 per cent in the number of support assistant hours allocated to pupils with SEN in mainstream schools in Wiltshire between 1983 and 1989. At the same time, inclusive practices in some LEAs resulted in the arrival of children with more severe difficulties than before. With them came specialist teachers and support assistants managed by central support services (O'Grady 1990) or providing outreach from special schools.

More recently, tight financial controls, growing class sizes, heavy curriculum and assessment demands and ever more children deemed to have special educational needs, have resulted in increasing numbers of classroom assistants being employed by schools themselves, particularly in the primary sector. As one head teacher, quoted by Moyles (1997) comments, 'No teacher minds having an extra two or three children in the class if they can have full-time support'.

According to recent government statistics (DfE 1994b), the number of educational support staff in primary schools rose from 13,641 in 1991 to 21,914 in 1994, while the number of primary teachers fell from 176,295 to 175,270. Although no comparable figures exist for the secondary sector, the Green Paper *Excellence for All Children* (DfEE 1997a) gives a figure of over 24,000 learning support assistants in mainstream primary and secondary schools and almost 16,000 in maintained special schools. A recent HMI Report (DES 1992) even found some large secondary schools who were considering phasing out the third deputy head in order to employ more ancillary staff.

Aims of support

In considering what is meant by support, Dyer (1988) tries to analyse the tasks performed by support workers. He classifies support under three main headings:

1. direct one-to-one pupil support,
2. teacher/pupil support, and
3. support in curriculum delivery.

In most primary schools, and increasingly at secondary level, one-to-one pupil support is provided by learning support assistants employed specifically for the purpose. Pothecary and McCarthy (1996) define this role in terms of:

- being familiar with one pupil's needs;
- running individual programmes;
- raising self-esteem;
- encouraging autonomy;
- having the time to foster self-determination;
- supporting a group while keeping one pupil's needs paramount;
- furthering the development of individual education plans (IEP) targets;
- adapting materials, and
- supporting work in subject areas.

In the secondary school, direct support may also be offered by a special needs teacher who has a particular range of relevant skills not possessed by the class or subject teacher. Such teachers may be part of the school's own support department or may come from an LEA support service. This level of support tends to be concentrated on those pupils with statements of special educational need and the role of the support teacher is often restricted by the demands of the statement.

However, this model has some of the same drawbacks as withdrawal and in many LEAs is being phased out in favour of more flexible teacher/pupil support, where the support worker supports both the pupils and the teacher. Again, different types of support worker can be involved and, as a consequence, the nature of the partnership will vary from one setting to another. Students can be offered support in a variety of ways (see Figure 1.1).

SUPPORTING CHILDREN

1. As members of the whole class:
   (a) responding to individual requests
   (b) managing behaviour
   (c) providing praise and encouragement

2. As members of a small group in class:
   (a) keeping pupils on task
   (b) explaining task requirements
   (c) supporting written work

3. As individuals in class:
   (a) acting as a scribe
   (b) delivering a structured programme
   (c) emotional or behavioural support

4. As members of a small withdrawal group:
   (a) delivering differentiated or structured curricular materials, e.g. corrective reading
   (b) discussing problems
   (c) delivering specific group programmes, e.g. social skills activities

5. As individuals on a withdrawal basis:
   (a) delivering structured learning programmes
   (b) delivering specific therapy programmes or medical procedures
   (c) individual counselling

Figure 1.1

Where this is being provided by an unqualified support assistant or a volunteer parent, the lead will come from the class or subject teacher, with the helper providing an extra pair of hands, eyes or ears. Teachers able to call on qualified nursery nurses or support assistants with additional training, such as the Certificate in Learning Support or a Specialist Teaching Assistant (STA) course, can share more of the load. In such cases, the role can include the preparation of teaching materials and the observation and recording of pupil behaviours, as well as greater involvement in the planning process.

As McNamara and Moreton (1993) note, 'children with special needs cannot simply be placed in a mainstream setting in the hope that normality will rub off on them'. To help ensure that their self-esteem is raised and their learning maximised, a properly planned programme of support is required. Before this can be done, it is vital that schools are clear about why they believe that support will make a difference and what form that support should take. In some settings, two adults are required to manage the class as a whole. At other times, there is a small group of pupils that need additional help. However, it must not be forgotten that in some circumstances support can in fact be counterproductive, stigmatising children or compounding their low self-esteem.

In determining the support needs of individuals or small groups, it is important to consult not only the professionals involved, but also the parents and the children themselves. As Wade and Moore (1993) stress, learning has more to do with the understandings and interpretations of students than with the intentions of their teachers. They emphasise the importance of allowing children to be actively involved in expressing their needs and in negotiating and setting objectives. In this way they are likely to have a more certain knowledge of their own strengths and weaknesses and thus to be more likely to value their successes.

In reviewing the development of in-class support in the secondary school, Bibby (1990) comments that one of the main reasons why schools began to move away from withdrawal models of remediation was the perceptions of the students concerned, who reported being picked on and called names. On the other hand, insensitive in-class support can be equally stigmatising and many pupils, particularly those of secondary age, resent being minded, preferring to seek help when they need it. This is particularly true in disadvantaged areas where students appear to be more sensitive to the risk of being singled out by too much individual attention (Duffield 1998).

Support staff in classrooms have an important role to play not only in supporting students but also in supporting teachers (see Figure 1.2). By so doing they can improve the educational opportunities for the entire class. For some teachers, the greatest support is afforded by colleagues who can devote time to modify teaching materials, prepare specific activities before the start of the lesson or keep a detailed record of behaviour and learning outcomes as the lesson progresses. Others value sharing the load of classroom management and feel more in control when they are offered an extra pair of eyes and ears to spot problems before they get out of hand.

> **SUPPORTING TEACHERS**
>
> 1. In teaching the class:
>   (a) covering for absence or course attendance
>   (b) team teaching
>   (c) taking one group, e.g. the most able
>
> 2. In managing the class:
>   (a) providing an extra pair of eyes and ears
>   (b) taking a share of student demands for help
>   (c) offering support and advice on management strategies
>
> 3. In differentiating materials:
>   (a) word-processing modified worksheets
>   (b) photocopying appropriate materials
>   (c) providing lists of subject specific key words
>
> 4. In managing resources:
>   (a) laying out the classroom before the lesson
>   (b) collecting apparatus from another colleague or the library
>   (c) assessing the readability level of textbooks or worksheets
>
> 5. In record keeping:
>   (a) completing a reading record of individual students
>   (b) filling in observation schedules
>   (c) assessing specific skills for review meetings

Figure 1.2

Some are happy to recognise their limited expertise in the special needs area and welcome the opportunity to learn from someone with more specialised knowledge. For others, the possibility of team teaching with a colleague who can share ideas and if necessary cover for absence or attendance at courses, without disrupting the smooth progress of the term's work, is the ideal. Nevertheless as Jordan (1994) notes, the process of classroom collaboration is a complex one requiring a high level of skill and sensitivity. Many teachers are fearful that they will be perceived as incompetent or will lay themselves open to criticism or blame. Others worry that requests for help will result in an increased workload instead of a speedy solution to their difficulties. Teachers seeking support do not want to be 'taken over' as a result of their request (Smith 1982); they need to share control of the problem.

Patterns of employment

In the special school sector, the presence of support teachers is unusual, although support assistants may constitute nearly half of the total staff complement. In some settings they even outnumber the teachers and, as budgets get tighter, the proportion of staff without a recognised qualification is increasing even further (Male 1996b). Despite this trend, most special schools still prefer to appoint staff with a nursery nursing or equivalent form of training behind them, particularly in the early years, and this has been equally true of those in the mainstream. In some LEAs, union agreements still prevent the appointment of support staff without a recognised form of training, the unions insisting for example that all LSAs are qualified nursery nurses. However, in others, schools have progressively responded to increasing class size and the challenge of resourcing special needs by employing support assistants from a wide range of educational backgrounds (Baskind and Thompson 1995).

Unqualified bilingual language assistants are found in many multiracial schools, particularly in inner-city LEAs able to attract Section 11 funding. They tend, in most cases, to be retained centrally as part of the service for EAL. However, increasingly, bilingual staff are being encouraged to train as nursery nurses or teachers and seek employment in generic services.

Even where longstanding union agreements exist, as in Bury, there is now a growing recognition that the standard NNEB training course is not necessarily that best suited to those working with older pupils or supporting children with particular disabilities. In many of these cases, a nursing qualification or experience in youth work, for example, is clearly more relevant. The Association for All Speech-Impaired Children (AFASIC) recommends that all support staff working with language-impaired pupils should have a minimum training to NVQ Level 3 in Communication Studies (AFASIC 1996). Similarly, many LEAs insist that assistants supporting students with hearing or visual impairments are additionally trained in British Sign Language (BSL) or Braille (RNIB 1994). Often these staff are retained centrally as part of the sensory support service, even where the responsibility for other assistants has been devolved to schools.

In many secondary schools, governors and senior managers have traditionally favoured the appointment of qualified teachers to carry out the support role (Lovey 1995). However, secondary schools are also beginning to recognise the advantages of a mixed economy and are recruiting support assistants to work alongside teachers in the classroom (Vincent *et al.* 1995). Not only is this seen as a good use of scarce resources, but it often allows schools to free up qualified teachers to work in a more focused way with individuals or small groups, as well as giving them time to develop appropriately differentiated teaching materials. While this approach has its merits, it is important that secondary schools also retain access to a pool of qualified and experienced support teachers.

This is particularly important with LEAs increasingly devolving funds to schools both for children on Stages 1–3 of the Code of Practice and for those with statements. Once the money has been handed over, there is rarely the wherewithal for LEAs to retain a significant number of peripatetic teachers or LSAs in a central pool upon whom schools can call. While it is generally more productive for schools to deploy their own specialist staff, who can be used more flexibly in response to changing needs, not all schools have access to appropriate levels of expertise from within their own staffing complement. In such circumstances, some have collaborated with their neighbours to share provision, a move to be encouraged in the face of the competitiveness of the last decade.

A recent survey by OFSTED (1996) helps to clarify the current position. In a study of 105 primary and 38 secondary schools across 33 LEAs they noted that:

1. There is less Special Support Assistant (SSA) support at secondary than at primary level, while the amount of teacher support increases across the key stages.
2. With few exceptions, only teacher support made a positive impact on standards of achievement.
3. SSA support is markedly more effective at primary level, perhaps because liaison between teachers and support assistants is easier when fewer adults are involved.
4. The quality of support given by SSAs to pupils with physical impairments is generally good at both primary and secondary level.

In recruiting support assistants many schools have found real benefit in employing local mothers, often transferring them from previous jobs as lunchtime supervisors or 'lollipop ladies'. An understanding of the needs of the community and an empathy with young people from the locality is often seen as a real asset. Others, seeking a wider recruitment base, have benefited from the employment of men, prematurely retired or readjusting after redundancy, and from the energy of unemployed graduates and gap-year students considering teaching as a career (Cheminais 1997). In some areas, schools are able to recruit qualified teachers who have taken early retirement or who are seeking a gradual re-entry to the profession after a career break.

In most authorities, while nursery nurses are normally employed on a permanent basis, support assistants are generally on temporary, part-time contracts, linked to the funding for individual pupils (Fletcher-Campbell 1992). A few LEAs and schools, aware of the need for job security and continuity, are now employing assistants on a longer term or permanent basis. In some areas, such as Tameside, they are retained centrally, with specialist teachers, as part of a learning support team and deployed, at no cost to the school, in response to changing needs. In others, such as Waltham Forest (Nolan and Gersch 1996) they are bought in from the Psychological Service by schools using delegated funding.

This type of arrangement gives a greater measure of job security and provides opportunities for coordinated management and training. On the other hand, it can result in less flexible support and can leave the assistant or peripatetic teacher isolated from colleagues in the school. Shared line management between the school and an LEA support service can lead to confusion both for the support assistant and the class teacher (Sloper and Tyler 1992) as the LSA may be getting contradictory messages from two 'bosses'. Similarly, schools may find it difficult to deploy staff from a central service as they would like, for example where the LEA insists on withdrawal, while the school favours in-class support.

Support and training

Throughout the country, LEAs have developed different systems, each with its own special terminology. Thus there are Educational Care Officers in Derbyshire, Special Needs Assistants in Leeds, Special Support Assistants in Bury, Teaching Assistants in Essex and Integration Assistants in Birmingham. The DfEE in its Green Paper *Excellence for All Children* (DfEE 1997a) uses the term Learning Support Assistants, while the newly-formed organisation for support assistants goes under the name of CLASS. One common feature of LEAs, who now take this group of staff seriously, is a rejection of the title 'non-teaching assistant'.

In response to pressures from schools to take over responsibility for selecting and managing their own support staff, LEAs are increasingly devolving funding to individual schools, despite this leaving many staff increasingly insecure and unsupported. As Bone and Mason, two Integration Assistants in Birmingham comment (Bone and Mason 1994):

> There is a real need for support from other members of staff and outside agencies for the person most closely involved with the child. It is very easy to become isolated with a feeling of total responsibility for the child.

In the best LEAs, devolved funding is coupled with a system of LEA support and training, as well as a network of advice to schools and assistants seeking new appointments. Thus in Cambridgeshire, a support network has been established between primary, secondary and special schools educating children with Down's syndrome (Ward-Wilkinson, personal communication). As she notes, 'the Link provides support, advice and sharing practices between headteachers, teachers, special educational needs co-ordinators and learning support assistants'.

Alongside training for support assistants, some LEAs are now offering training in consultancy to peripatetic teachers, as well as training for SENCOs and class teachers, on ways of using support to best effect (Lorenz 1996). Regrettably, as Balshaw (1998) notes, the Department for Education and Employment (DfEE) fails to mention support assistants under 'colleagues to liaise with' in their latest handbook for SENCOs (DfEE 1997c) and thus misses a valuable opportunity to flag up the importance of management responsibility for effective support.

In the special school sector, staff almost invariably have the advantage of permanent full-time jobs. Nevertheless, as Mittler (1993) notes, opportunities for training and career development are still very limited. Throughout their excellent booklet on planning the curriculum for pupils with profound and multiple learning difficulties (SCAA 1996), the Schools Curriculum and Assessment Authority makes not one mention of care staff, nursery nurses or support assistants. Although they stress the need for multidisciplinary teamwork, a consistency of approach by different staff and the involvement of all staff in the planning process, no attempt is made to consider the unique role of the school's support assistants.

While the majority of special school head teachers believe that they value their support assistants and teachers equally, discussions with support assistants in some schools gives a very different picture. Patterns of discrimination go far beyond the salary and status differentials; most ancillary staff experience significantly different conditions of service from teaching staff, often working over breaks and lunchtimes or acting as bus escorts at either end of the school day. Opportunities for training and career progression are often restricted or non-existent and relatively few feel that they are able to influence policies or practice within the organisation. Where schools have addressed the needs of this significant group of staff, both job satisfaction and effectiveness have increased markedly.

Notwithstanding the undoubted growth in the use of support assistants in classrooms, there have been those who have advised caution. De Vault et al. (1977) noted that the presence of additional personnel did not automatically improve the learning environment. Rather than freeing teachers to increase productive contact with children, the presence of an auxiliary merely gave them more time for administrative tasks. HMI in their survey of non-teaching staff (DES 1992), note: 'The effectiveness of many was constrained to a greater or lesser degree by factors which included a limited perception, on the part of schools and these staff themselves, of their capabilities and potential'.

Mortimore et al. (1994) in their study, found the presence of auxiliary staff in schools led senior management teams to pay particular attention to issues of role, status and professional boundaries. Nevertheless, as Lorenz (1996) notes (see Figure 1.3), assistants regularly express concern about a wide range of issues.

For support teachers (Lovey 1995) the problems, although just as real, relate more to teamwork, joint planning and communication with subject staff. Nevertheless, support teachers funded via statements are subject to just the same job insecurities as support assistants and many complain in the same way about poorly-defined roles and responsibilities, the lack of a proper job description, low status and a lack of support. If support teachers and classroom assistants are to be used effectively it is imperative that these key issues are addressed by LEAs and by schools. Similarly, where schools are considering using parents in a support role, careful thought and planning are required (McQuillan 1987).

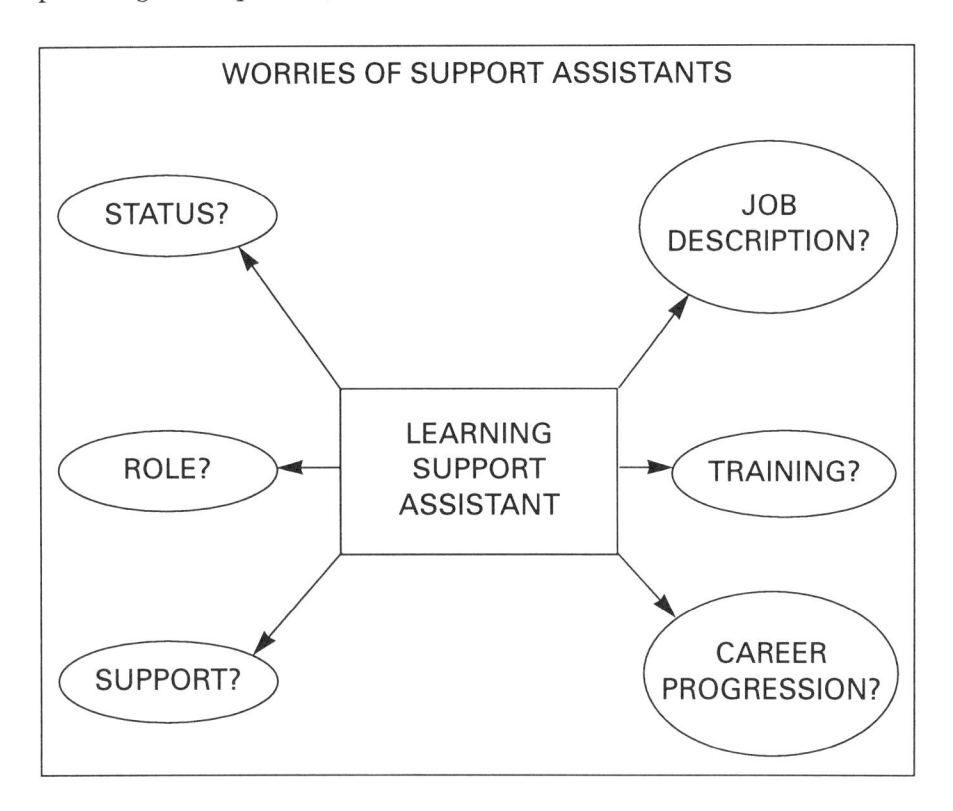

```
WORRIES OF SUPPORT ASSISTANTS

   STATUS?                              JOB DESCRIPTION?

   ROLE?  ←——  LEARNING SUPPORT ASSISTANT  ——→  TRAINING?

   SUPPORT?                             CAREER PROGRESSION?
```

Figure 1.3

Chapter 2

Meeting Children's Needs

Traditionally, slow-learning pupils in mainstream schools were withdrawn from normal lessons and taught separately for all or part of their time. However, the advent of the Warnock Report (DES 1978), together with the widespread acceptance of the comprehensive system and mixed ability teaching, led many schools to adopt a more inclusive philosophy and to favour in-class support. The introduction of the National Curriculum gave further impetus to this movement, as it was no longer permissible to deny pupils access to subjects such as French in order to reinforce skills in basic literacy or numeracy.

While special classes still exist in some places and many schools still group their pupils by ability or withdraw children periodically for specific purposes, most pupils with learning difficulties are now supported in mixed-ability classes for much of their time. In the worst case scenario, no attempt is made by the class or subject teacher to modify either the content of the curriculum or the way in which it is delivered. Instead the teacher relies on an extra adult who is often reduced to coaxing pupils through a lesson which they are barely capable of comprehending (Audit Commission 1992). In the majority of cases, however, teachers will differentiate both the lesson content and the method of presentation used. Prior planning should enable the adults involved to select appropriate materials or prepare an approach which will enable all pupils to follow the lesson.

By using support staff to develop and modify resources, instead of sitting next to pupils telling them the answers, the pupil with learning difficulties is helped to become an independent learner and the support worker is freed up to support other pupils. As the Audit Commission (1992) notes, support through preparation and planning does not isolate the pupil socially from his or her peers. This is particularly important where individual children have been allocated their own support assistant for up to 30 hours a week, as is the case for many pupils with Down's syndrome in mainstream schools.

A recent survey by the author (Lorenz 1998a) indicates that in nearly half of the responses received, the assistant sits beside the child most of the

Supporting slow learners

time, rarely helping other children in the class. Where the assistant is 'Velcro'd' to the child, there is a real danger that the child will be prevented from forming relationships with his or her peers and will develop a dependency on the support worker which may be difficult to break.

Children used to their own personal 'slave' may resent sharing the support with others in the class or may feel unable to initiate an activity without the permission of their assistant. These children then begin to believe that they can only produce good quality work when there is an adult sitting beside them, attributing success to the adult rather than to their own efforts. This learned helplessness (Skaalvik 1990) ensures that they stop work as soon as their support assistant or teacher moves away, but start up again the minute they return.

In addition to a well-differentiated curriculum, the child with learning difficulties in the mainstream classroom is likely to benefit from individual help, which may be difficult for even the best teacher to deliver consistently. Pre-teaching of key concepts or vocabulary can allow children to take part in a lesson on an equal footing with their peers. This is often far more beneficial than going over work once they have experienced failure.

As McNamara and Moreton (1993) point out, concentrating for too long on children's areas of weakness may lead them to become less well motivated and to develop avoidance strategies to reduce the risk of further failure. Helping children access back-up materials, such as word lists or dictionaries, can enable them to complete tasks themselves without the need for adult intervention.

While the work offered may be well suited to the ability of the child, many pupils still find it difficult to sit still and concentrate, and will require direction or prompting if they are not to disturb others in the class. A good support teacher or assistant can bring the child back to task and reward appropriate behaviour without creating dependency. Reassurance and encouragement, particularly when new tasks are presented, can be vital if the child is to succeed. Where the child is also a second language learner, the presence of a support worker who speaks their mother tongue can be an enormous asset. In the same way, a support worker who can sign is likely to be far more effective in gaining the confidence of a deaf or language-delayed child than one who struggles to understand what the child is trying to say. In supporting the child with learning difficulties Caswell and Pinner (1996) make a number of recommendations (see Figure 2.1).

Finally, the issue of skill development needs to be addressed. For certain children, targeted support from an unqualified classroom assistant, in a group or in a mixed-ability setting within the classroom, is sufficient to ensure the development of basic skills. For many others, however, more focused teaching is required. In some instances, the presence of a qualified nursery nurse or support teacher in the classroom will significantly increase the probability of the child receiving appropriately skilled input. Alternatively, class teachers may use an assistant or support teacher to keep the class working quietly, freeing them to work with an individual or small group themselves.

SUPPORTING THE SLOW LEARNER

1. Help the child work as independently as possible in class.

2. Allow the child to work as far as possible with the same materials and engage in the same activities as the rest of the class.

3. Ensure that Individual Education Plans (IEPs) relate to real, relevant and realistic classroom goals.

4. Allow the child to practise and demonstrate newly acquired skills.

Figure 2.1

Supporting children with specific learning difficulties

Until quite recently, many children with specific learning difficulties (SpLD), were considered to be slow learners and were placed in remedial classes or bottom sets. Others were viewed as lazy or uncooperative and punished for their illegible handwriting or failure to produce homework. Pupils we now consider to have specific difficulties were often subjected to sarcastic comments from unsympathetic teachers, or were made to stay behind to repeat poorly completed work, without any real attempt being made to understand their difficulties or acknowledge their underlying intelligence.

Fortunately this is no longer the case in most parts of the country, and pupils with dyslexia, dyspraxia, attention deficit disorder (ADD) or a range of other specific difficulties are being identified at an increasingly early stage in their educational career. However, this presents major problems for many teachers and parents who feel that a diagnosis should result in individualised input from a specially trained teacher.

For the small proportion of SpLD students with statements, many LEAs still offer the traditional diet of one or two hours teaching per week on a withdrawal basis, provided by a teacher from a central support service. However, it is becoming increasingly apparent that for those students with less severe difficulties, skill teaching outside the classroom is not the answer. Even for those pupils requiring such focused input, additional in-class support is necessary if they are to access the curriculum at an appropriate level. As Lovey (1995) comments, 'Children with specific learning difficulties are the pupils who are most likely to need support in mainstream classrooms'.

Without support, many secondary-aged students are faced with a choice between struggling in a middle or top set without additional help, or languishing in a bottom set bored and unstimulated. In a higher set, the work is likely to be at an appropriate level to provide an intellectual challenge, but could present major problems in terms of accessing written materials and recording outcomes. In a bottom set, the literacy demands will be reduced, but the student may be placed with students of limited ability or who present behavioural problems.

Even in the primary school or in a mixed-ability setting at secondary level, help with reading, writing, self-management and the completion of practical tasks may be essential if children with specific difficulties are to achieve their true potential. Often these children have experienced a period of frustration and failure before their difficulties have been recognised. Hence, for many, problems of low self-esteem remain; many pupils are poorly motivated and feel that success is beyond their reach. Others use their difficulties as an excuse not to persevere and need considerable prompting and encouragement if they are to make progress.

In some LEAs, in-class support is provided by SpLD teachers who spend part of their time working alongside students in the classroom, as well as teaching on a withdrawal basis. By so doing, they are able to discover what difficulties the pupils are facing in normal classes and modify their input accordingly. In addition they are able to advise class teachers on alternative forms of record-keeping that students might use, e.g.

- tape recording,
- using a lap-top or word processor,
- developing the use of pictorial records through cartoons or photos,
- peer collaboration with a good writer who has fewer bright ideas, or
- dictating to a peer or a volunteer adult.

They can advise on ways of improving a student's organisational skills and remind teachers about the difficulties faced by many students in copying down from the board or writing at speed, even when they appear to have legible writing. A support teacher can use a range of strategies to improve the performance of individual students. In the secondary school context, Lovey (1995) mentions:

1. reading the first paragraph aloud while the student looks at the text, before tackling it themselves,
2. assessing the difficulty of a text by using the 'finger test' before giving it to the student to read. The student chooses a passage from the middle of the book and starts reading it. The little finger is placed on the first word the student cannot read, the ring finger on the next failed word and so on. If the student runs out of fingers on one hand before getting to the bottom of the page, the text is too difficult,
3. reading a set text onto tape for the student to study via a tape recorder and headphones,
4. encouraging the student to prepare a quiz on the text he or she has just read,
5. writing down the student's story or essay in pencil for them to go over later or at home when they have more time,
6. pointing out spelling errors and teaching spelling rules as the student completes classwork,

7. helping the student make notes, draft and redraft work before attempting the final version,
8. teaching techniques to prompt memory, e.g. letters on the back of the hand.

In some schools, much of this work is carried out by LSAs trained by a central service or by the school. As time goes on and awareness of the difficulties faced by students in the classroom grows, more LEAs are offering pupils with statements a mixed diet of specialist teacher and LSA support, or moving them after a period of qualified teacher input onto in-class support from a support assistant. Schools with their own support teachers or LSAs are increasingly offering in-class support for students at Stages 2 and 3 of the Code of Practice, as well as providing small-group skill teaching and this has immeasurably increased the performance of a whole range of students with SpLD.

Supporting children with physical difficulties

Since the turn of the century or even earlier, most children with physical difficulties of any magnitude have been placed in special schools or units. However, mainstream placements are now becoming increasingly common as local authorities adopt barrier-free policies backed up by input from the relevant health authority. Following on from a survey of five LEAs (Coopers and Lybrand 1992) which reviewed access to the mainstream for pupils with physical disabilities, government funding to improve access to schools has now been made available.

As a consequence, increasing numbers of disabled children are able to attend their local mainstream school or one specially adapted by the LEA. With such a large and diverse population, schools need to address a whole range of issues before they are able to provide an appropriate support package for an individual child (see Figure 2.2).

Helen Kenward, in her excellent book *Integrating Pupils with Disabilities in Mainstream Schools* (Kenward 1997), lists several different types of support which might be required:

1. One-to-one support for a pupil with a severe disability, such as in the later stages of muscular dystrophy. Here a pupil might need help in:
   (a) communication, using a communication device such as the Light Talker or a symbol system;
   (b) recording work, the assistant acting as a scribe or helping with word processing or the use of a dictaphone.
2. *Support in practical tasks*. Support staff are invaluable in lessons such as Music, Art, Physical Education or Technology to ensure that the student plays a full part.
3. *Acting as a reader, interpreter or prompter*. This type of help may be needed for a pupil with a visual or hearing impairment or one with a speech and language disorder.

> **SUPPORT FOR CHILDREN WITH PHYSICAL DISABILITIES**
>
> 1. Does the child have access or mobility difficulties which require the provision of mobility aids or building adaptations? ☐
>
> 2. Will adult help be required in addition to that provided by the class teacher or by peers? ☐
>
> 3. Does the child have medical problems which require the administration of medication? ☐
>
> 4. Is the child likely to miss school on a regular basis because of ill health or hospital appointments? ☐
>
> 5. Do staff require training in particular procedures such as dealing with an epileptic fit, clearing a blocked drainage tube, checking a hearing aid or changing a colostomy bag? ☐
>
> 6. Does the child have additional learning difficulties? ☐
>
> 7. Are there staffing or resource implications for any necessary interventions? ☐
>
> 8. Is the child seen regularly by a speech or physiotherapist in school? ☐
>
> 9. Will support staff be required to implement therapy programmes? ☐
>
> 10. Will support staff need particular skills such as Braille or British Sign Language? ☐
>
> 11. If so, is appropriate training available? ☐

Figure 2.2

    4. *Assisting with personal care needs.* This may include help with toileting, dressing and personal hygiene. Above all, the aim must be to help students achieve independence, while respecting their privacy and treating them with dignity and respect. Wherever possible, students should be offered support in intimate tasks from staff of the same sex, particularly at secondary level. Failing this, a same-sex peer should always be available to mediate.

    5. *Assisting with physical care.* Students with physical disabilities frequently require regular physiotherapy, speech and language therapy or occupational therapy. Support staff are often required

to carry out programmes devised by a therapist. In some instances staff may need to carry out procedures such as postural drainage or support students in a walker or standing frame. In all these areas supervision and training are essential.
6. *Small group work*. While many children with physical disabilities function within normal limits, others have significant learning difficulties which need to be addressed. Such help may include:
   (a) in-class support to help pupils access the curriculum or remain on task;
   (b) withdrawal support, working on a teacher-directed activity;
   (c) observation of student learning and behaviour. Support staff standing back to watch what is actually going on in lessons can assist the class teacher to make appropriate modifications to the lesson content or form of presentation.

For the student with a physical disability in a mainstream setting, the primary aim of support must be to help them become as independent as possible. One way in which this can be achieved, is to create an environment in which students support each other; students who have been supported primarily by peers appear to cope better in adult life. Rather than providing direct help to the child, staff can encourage and support natural alliances, e.g. helping the child move around the building, take part in practical activities such as science or participate in PE lessons. Approaches such as Circle Time (Curry and Broomfield 1994) or the development of circles of friends (Wilson and Newton 1996) can make a useful contribution to the involvement of peers.

Where support staff are required, their role should, wherever possible, be to remain one step behind, allowing the child to take calculated risks. As Fox (1993) comments:

> It is a difficult task to maintain the balance between giving support and promoting independence. This involves being clear about your expectations and firm in your directions without pressurising the child. However, sensitivity should tell you if and when to intervene.

Ensuring the safety of the child, without overprotecting or doing too much for them, can be difficult for some people. As teachers speaking on the recent CSIE tape (Shaw 1997) remark, support assistants need to be sensitive to children's needs, but must take care not to undermine their ability to think for themselves. Physical needs must not be confused with mental needs and action must be taken to avoid the child becoming lazy and handing over too much responsibility to a care assistant.

If disabled students are to gain confidence as independent members of the school community, it is important for everyone to treat them in the same way as any other pupil of the same age. They also need to be permitted to talk for themselves and make their own choices. Wherever possible, this should extend to involvement in the determination of IEP targets, participation in annual reviews and even to the definition of their support assistant's role. As one articulate young wheelchair-user (Mason, personal communication) states in the job description she drew up for her new support assistant (see Figure 2.3) she 'must understand that the child knows their disability best'.

JOB DESCRIPTION
Musts and must nots

1. Must be a woman.

2. Must be young enough to understand a young person's mind.

3. Must have a strong back and strong arms.

4. Must be able to listen to what child wants and use their say (the child's say) whenever possible.

5. Must know the *limits* of keeping a child safe.

6. Must understand that the child knows their disability best.

7. Must let child make judgement on what's safe and what's not for her.

8. Must not have a tendency to get ill regularly.

9. Must not want job for power.

10. Must be willing to stay after school (you do get paid £).

11. Must be able to stop older students who the child feels is endangering them.

12. Must let the child decide on things they like, where they want to go and when.

I will need a helper to come to and from school with me.
I will need a helper at break and at lunch.
I will need a helper to come to PE lessons and technology and going to the loo.
I will need a helper for some after-school clubs.
I won't need a helper for changing lessons on most occasions.

Figure 2.3

Supporting children with emotional and behavioural problems

Many children, particularly those with learning or physical difficulties, display behaviours that cause concern to school staff. The reasons underlying these behaviours can be varied and complex and so a range of different strategies may need to be used in different situations. While close liaison between the class teacher and the support staff is always important, consistency of approach is essential when attempts are being made to change children's behaviour. A well-thought-out whole-school behaviour policy and clear class rules can be a great help to adults and children alike.

Effective classroom management by the class or subject teacher can prevent many problems occurring in the first place and can minimise the impact of those that do. Nevertheless, the behaviour of some individuals or groups of children will present a challenge to even the best organised teacher. In these cases, the presence of another adult can be of immense value.

Support can take a variety of forms including a second adult:

- to share the responsibility for monitoring behaviour and nipping problems in the bud;
- to increase the adult/child ratio and thus the amount of positive attention each child can receive;
- responsible for giving regular praise and encouragement to particular children, while the class teacher takes responsibility for the learning programme;
- who can remove individual children from the room and allow them to calm down without disrupting the class.

However, as Wade and Moore (1993) note, just managing children's behaviour without attempting to understand their feelings can be a dangerous course to follow. Pothecary and McCarthy (1996) in their training pack for support assistants, stress the need to hear the child's version of events before intervening. Thus support for children with emotional problems can also involve a person who:

- can befriend the child and help build trust;
- has the time to listen to the child and understand his or her point of view;
- can withdraw the child for individual counselling sessions;
- is available to work with a small group on developing social skills or raising self-esteem.

Teaching a disturbed or disturbing child can be particularly stressful for even the most experienced teacher. The support of a classroom assistant or support teacher can be particularly valuable in maintaining a sense of calm order in the classroom, implementing a consistent management strategy and injecting some humour into the situation. This is particularly the case in a special school or unit where large numbers of pupils might be exhibiting challenging behaviour.

In implementing and evaluating any management programme, detailed record-keeping is essential. In many schools, support staff are used to observe children's behaviour and keep a diary, complete an observation schedule or record the frequency of certain categories of behaviour (Lorenz 1998b). Samples of behaviour taken at different times or in different situations can help the class teacher or the other professionals involved to understand the causes of undesirable behaviours and develop more effective ways of reducing their frequency or severity.

Where children are thought to be at risk of neglect or sexual abuse, support staff may be the first to notice any changes in behaviour or mood. These observations can be used to alert relevant professionals and ensure appropriate help is offered. Support assistants who have developed a trusting relationship with a child are often the first to be told about bullying or abuse and need to be clear what action to take. Of particular importance is the need to distinguish between those pieces of information which can be kept a secret between the assistant and the child and those which must be passed on to the school's Child Protection Coordinator.

Schools that can call on an experienced teacher from their own support department or from an LEA behaviour support team to work alongside teachers in the classroom, have access to a range of additional strategies. By acting in a consultative capacity as Hanko (1995) observes: 'the consultant supplements the consultee's expertise with his own, thereby helping highlight the issues underlying the case to be explored and enabling the consultee to arrive at new solutions'.

As Hockley (1985) notes, a good support teacher can offer a whole range of skills (see Figure 2.4). They can:

- help reduce the teacher's anxiety about the child's problem;
- observe the class and provide feedback on management strategies, working collaboratively to develop an intervention package;
- teach the class, allowing the class teacher to observe the behaviour of individuals or groups;

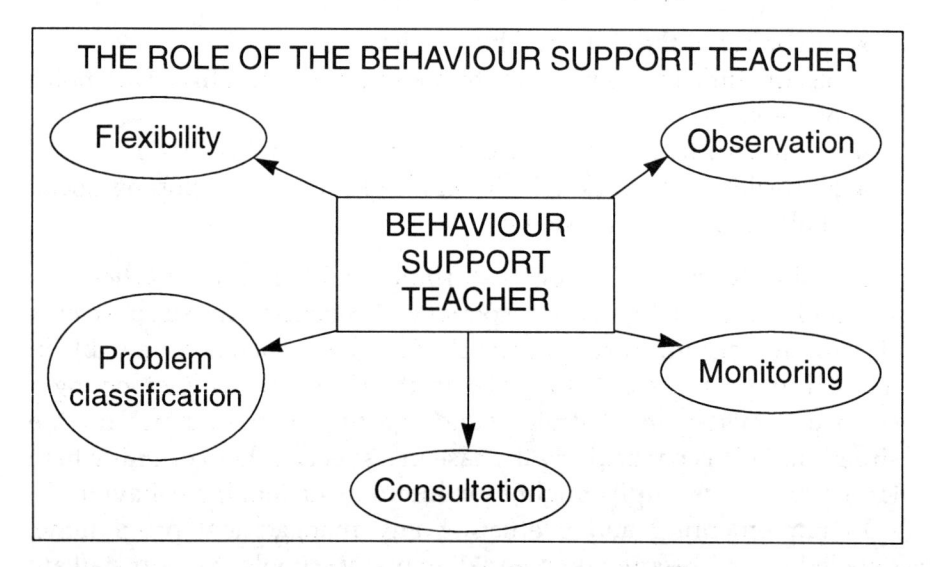

Figure 2.4

- demonstrate particular approaches such as Circle Time (Curry and Broomfield 1994) which the teacher can take part in and can subsequently introduce into the curriculum;
- teach cooperatively with the class teacher, modelling positive ways of dealing with undesirable behaviours.

Hopefully, over time, in-class support for children with behaviour problems can be phased out as the young people concerned feel appreciated, begin to succeed in school and gain in self-esteem.

Chapter 3
Support in the Primary School

Nursery nurses are trained, via the Certificate or Diploma in Nursery Nursing of the National Nursery Examination Board (NNEB) or an equivalent BTech or NVQ qualification, to work with children from birth to seven years of age. Increasingly, however, qualified nursery nurses are being employed in mainstream and special schools to support children of junior or even of secondary age. In such circumstances additional training is essential.

In the HMI survey of non-teaching staff (DES 1992) qualified nursery assistants were found to carry out an enormous range of duties (see Figure 3.1). While working as autonomous professionals, nursery nurses in school remain under the direction of the teacher at all times. Despite this, the teacher and nursery nurse should always see themselves as a team, with complementary roles. As Bruce (1987) comments, both partners need each other. Their duties, while distinct and separate, should be overlapping and integrated.

Le Laurin and Risley (1972), studying staff roles in day-care settings, came to the conclusion that deploying staff in particular areas or 'zones', dealing with a throughput of children, was more effective than allocating them to their own group. Whatever the approach employed, the teacher must retain overall responsibility for all staff. As Johnston (1984) discovered, it is this aspect of the job that nursery teachers find the most stressful, particularly safeguarding sufficient time to adequately supervise colleagues. In a survey of 291 nursery teachers in the USA (summarised in Lorenz 1998a: 26) more problems were reported in this area of work than in any other.

Although the salary differential implies a hierarchical relationship, it is important that the nursery nurse is not relegated to a menial role, undertaking the most irksome aspects of the job, e.g. clearing up after children, rather than extending their learning. A growing shortage of teachers with dedicated early years training is likely to render the expertise of the nursery nurse of increasing importance as strategies to reduce class size are enacted. If teachers fail to recognise the important contribution that nursery nurse colleagues are able to make in

The role of the nursery nurse

> **THE ROLE OF THE NURSERY NURSE**
>
> - Help plan the work of the class
> - Prepare and maintain materials and equipment
> - Mount and display children's work
> - Organise the classroom
> - Maintain contact with parents
> - Supervise children and assist them with a wide range of work
> - Facilitate group work
> - Assist groups in practical activities such as painting or science
> - Help with language and maths
> - Hear children read
> - Supervise the use of apparatus
> - Report children's achievements to the teacher
> - Help keep records of children's progress

Figure 3.1

facilitating children's learning, then a valuable resource will be wasted.

The role of adults in fostering the development of young children is very different from that of the teacher working within the strictures of the National Curriculum (Lloyd 1997). This distinction is clearly established in the training of the nursery nurse who is encouraged to:

- begin with the learning processes of the child;
- recognise different rates of development;
- start with what the child can do rather than what he or she cannot do;
- act as an enabler, structuring and managing a stimulating and challenging learning environment;
- emphasise opportunities for creativity and play;
- facilitate a rich variety of personal interactions.

As the experience of nursery nurses and teachers working together has increased, the role of the nursery nurse has expanded. Many schools have updated their original job descriptions to recognise the greater involvement of qualified nursery nurses in planning and curriculum delivery. A growing awareness of special educational needs and the move towards earlier identification has led schools increasingly to use their nursery nurses to support individuals or small groups of pupils experiencing particular difficulties.

Only a small number of children with significant disabilities are assessed preschool and come into nursery or reception with a statement of special educational need. Instead, nursery staff are increasingly being expected to assess children while providing them with an appropriate educational experience. Without the support of the nursery nurses already in post, this would not be possible. Nevertheless, their existence is often used as the means by which LEAs can check their special needs expenditure, delaying the assessment process and hence the provision of additional resources until the child enters school on a full-time basis.

Where qualified nursery nurses are employed specifically to support an individual child via statement funding, their role is in theory no different from that of the unqualified LSA. Nevertheless, for many schools, the presence of a qualified early years professional adds significantly to the quality of support that can be offered. NNEB-trained support assistants are more likely to realise when the child is no longer benefiting from the provision being made and when the programme needs to be modified. They are likely to have a wider range of skills that can be applied in the learning situation and should be less reliant on the supervision of the teacher.

On the other hand, for the teacher with little commitment to children with special educational needs and few skills in differentiation, handing over total responsibility to the nursery nurse is all too easy. The outcome can be a child with significant learning needs, who has no input from a qualified teacher and who may be taught in isolation from his or her peers. Outcomes from a recent survey of children with Down's syndrome in mainstream primary schools (Lorenz 1998a), indicate that fewer than half such children receive input from their class teacher on a daily basis.

To avoid this problem, many schools now use the additional nursery nurse to increase their overall adult:child ratio, thus freeing the teacher to work with the special needs child, individually or in a small group, on a regular basis. While this role swap may be difficult or inappropriate with an unqualified support assistant, the use of support staff with early years training should allow maximum flexibility to the benefit of staff and children.

Working with classroom assistants

Classroom assistants are now a regular feature of the modern primary school. Used properly and well, a school's support assistants are an important and vital asset to the whole-school SEN team approach (Pothecary and McCarthy 1996). However, there is a lot more to their deployment than merely providing hard-pressed teachers with extra help. Research evidence (Thomas 1992), indicates that putting additional adults in a classroom is not, in itself, sufficient to improve the quality of educational experience available to the pupils. So how should support assistants be spending their time?

To a large extent this will depend on the terms under which the assistant has been appointed. Some assistants are employed directly by the school and paid out of the delegated budget, to provide general support across the school. Research by Rees (1995) indicates that such assistants perceive themselves as 'somewhere between a teacher and an auntie'. On the other hand, the teacher's view of these assistants is as 'a helper who follows the teacher's direction to the best of his/her ability'.

In some cases this has proved difficult where teacher and assistant do not 'click' and the assistant becomes preoccupied with satisfying the teacher. The qualities said to make a good assistant were defined by the head teachers in the study as the ability to:

- relate to staff
- drop everything and change plan
- listen and work within a framework.

Boundaries between the roles of the classroom assistant and the teacher are often poorly defined and vary from school to school and from teacher to teacher. However, Mortimore *et al.* (1994) found some common ground (see Figure 3.2). Although undoubtedly a boon to hard-pressed teachers, general classroom assistants are becoming less common as budgets are squeezed and the demands created by the SEN Code of Practice (DfEE 1994a) push schools into using their existing assistants to support pupils with special needs. Instead, schools are increasingly relying on parents and volunteers to carry out these less specific duties. Special needs assistants, on the other hand, are on the increase in many primary schools.

In most cases they are employed specifically to support a particular student. In some LEAs, such as Tameside, they are part of a central support team and come into school to work with their named child on an agreed basis. In other LEAs, such as Bury and Leeds, money is devolved to the school. Where schools have several statemented students, each allocated part-time support, hours can be pooled and assistants employed on a full-time basis. Not only does this allow schools to use support more flexibly and in response to changing need, but it gives assistants a more varied and secure job. As one child leaves, another generally arrives to take its place and the school is able to maintain experienced staff long term.

Whether support assistants are employed by an individual school or by the LEA, head teachers should take responsibility for their day-to-day management and help define the role they will undertake. However specific the statement, it is rarely in the interest of any child to have an assistant hovering over them the whole time. Schools, therefore, need to be flexible and creative in the way they use support

> **THE ROLE OF THE GENERAL CLASSROOM ASSISTANT**
>
> Assistants DO
>
> - Take groups of pupils, under teacher supervision
> - Reinforce and consolidate learning
> - Manage the children in their group
> - Record the children's performance
>
> They DO NOT
>
> - Teach the class as a whole
> - Initiate or plan activities
> - Assess the children's learning
> - Set standards of behaviour

Figure 3.2

and to impress upon LEA officers and parents that good inclusive practice is about building a bridge between the child and the curriculum, not about intensive one-to-one interventions.

Schools must feel confident that, by moving the assistant away from the child at times to increase independence, the amount of support will not be cut. On the other hand, LEAs must be reassured that schools will not keep support when the child no longer needs it or use staff inappropriately, e.g. assisting pupils in other classes. In determining a role for the support assistant, several factors need to be taken into consideration (see Figure 3.3).

The roles adopted by support assistants can be many and varied; yet all may be equally valid. Pupils with special educational needs can be supported in a variety of ways, either individually or in groups. However, the aims must be to:

- give the pupils access to as much of the normal lesson as possible;
- encourage the pupils to be as independent as possible;
- ensure that the pupils can gain some success;
- ensure that the pupils learn new skills or improve those already learnt;
- foster cooperative working and facilitate the development of friendships.

Some pupils may need access to an assistant throughout the day because of a severe mobility problem or the risk of fits. However, once

---

FACTORS TO CONSIDER

- The **needs of the SEN pupil** or pupils
- The **needs of other pupils** in the class
- The **type of lesson**
- The **methods used** by the class teacher
- The **skills** of the support assistant
- The **wishes** of the **teacher, assistant** and **child**

Figure 3.3

on-task, the child may cope perfectly well and the assistant will then be free to help others in the class. Some pupils need targeted help with learning a new skill or carrying out a practical task, but are capable of coping without help for the remainder of the time. As Fletcher-Campbell (1992) notes: 'not only is it a waste of a valuable resource if the classroom assistant remains with a pupil needlessly, but it also serves to highlight the difference between the pupil and his or her peers'.

A good support assistant will support not only the child or children with special educational needs, but will also play an important role in supporting their teacher. While many teachers are initially worried about having another adult in their classroom, most come to value the benefits it brings and would be loath to do without them. As Fletcher-Campbell (1992) notes, there can be few teachers who, in the course of an average week, do not long for an extra pair of hands. In taking on this role the support assistant must:

- remember that the teacher is responsible for all the children throughout the lesson;
- support the teacher at all times when there are pupils present;
- ask the teacher for guidance if the child is unhappy or can't cope with the work;
- give feedback to the teacher as often as possible.

The bilingual language assistant

Linguistic diversity is now the norm in many British classrooms, as we become an increasingly multicultural and multilingual society. Some pupils, whose first language is not English, will need help in developing their ability to speak, read and write the English language and in acquiring sufficient understanding of the underlying concepts and processes to be able to achieve success in school. Yet they may have no particular difficulty in their mother tongue and should not be considered to have SEN. On the other hand, some bilingual pupils also experience learning, physical or behavioural difficulties which need to be addressed alongside their language needs.

While historically children newly arrived in this country were placed in segregated language units (CRE 1986) until such time as they were considered to possess sufficient linguistic competence to manage in a local school, this practice has now been abandoned in favour of support within the mainstream curriculum. In the majority of schools there has been a further move away from the separate teaching of small groups on a withdrawal basis, or in one corner of the classroom, towards a more integrated approach (OFSTED 1994). This movement closely parallels the development of inclusive education for pupils with special educational needs and has occurred for the same fundamental reasons.

Experience in multiracial schools (Mills and Mills 1993), confirms the view that second language learning is aided by genuine contexts and the application of language skills to real-life problems. Gravelle (1996) suggests that what is required is the provision of focused support, which equips the student with a framework in which to become an independent learner, delivered within a rich multicultural environment. At the same time, pupils need the opportunity to use their first languages in the classroom.

The use of their mother tongue is both a confirmation of the worth of their culture and a real help in learning. For new entrants to this country, acceptance and use of their first language in school can ease the transition and help reduce feelings of alienation (Gibbons 1991). Research shows that children fluent in their own language find second language acquisition easier than those whose grasp of their mother tongue is still insecure (Cummins 1984). Grouping new language learners with outgoing and sociable peers sharing the same first language can be helpful, as long as this is not to the exclusion of pupils demonstrating good models of English.

The presence of a bilingual assistant in the classroom can aid both the monolingual teacher and the bilingual children in a variety of ways, as the handout from the Bury EAL Service shows (see Figure 3.4). To facilitate curriculum access, the bilingual assistant will need to work alongside the teacher, clarifying the curriculum for the target students. However, as Gravelle (1996) points out, it is important that this does not consist merely of translating instructions or providing appropriate English vocabulary. Further, it is essential that tasks are not simplified excessively, reducing the cognitive challenge of classroom activities. Instead instructions should be extended and amplified to achieve understanding. As a member of the classroom team, the bilingual assistant should be involved in curriculum planning and in assessment and record-keeping of the target pupils.

Much has been written about the value of bilingual assessment for early language learners. 'Without bilingual skills, teachers are trying to find the best high jumper by seeing who's good at running' (Mills

Effective In-class Support

The Bilingual Language Assistant

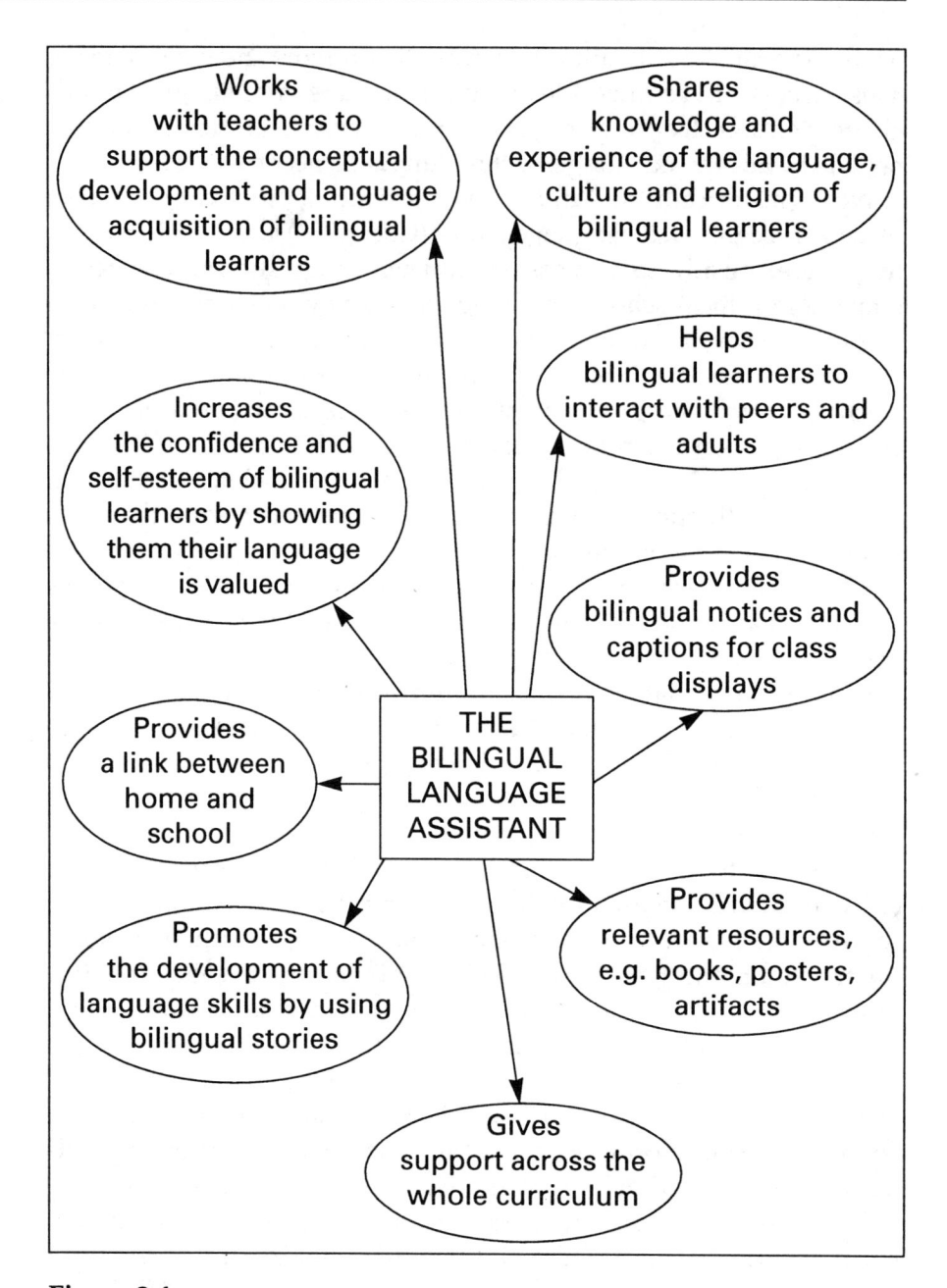

- Works with teachers to support the conceptual development and language acquisition of bilingual learners
- Shares knowledge and experience of the language, culture and religion of bilingual learners
- Helps bilingual learners to interact with peers and adults
- Increases the confidence and self-esteem of bilingual learners by showing them their language is valued
- Provides bilingual notices and captions for class displays
- Provides a link between home and school
- Provides relevant resources, e.g. books, posters, artifacts
- Promotes the development of language skills by using bilingual stories
- Gives support across the whole curriculum

Figure 3.4

and Mills 1993). On the other hand, mother tongue assessment can be both difficult and unreliable, particularly where the assessment is of skills taught in English. A bilingual assistant, faced with an assessment task, may have real difficulty in finding an appropriate technical word in the child's first language or a grammatical structure that conveys the same meaning as the English version.

On the other hand, mother tongue assessment of first language proficiency can be very useful. In her book *Assessing the Needs of Bilingual Pupils*, Hall (1995) includes a variety of school-based assessments which can be carried out by a bilingual assistant. When used flexibly alongside other forms of observation and assessment, these clearly have a place in any multiracial school's repertoire.

Meeting children's social and cultural needs can be a varied and multifaceted process. For the new arrival, the bilingual assistant may be the only person able to determine the root of a child's distress and be able to relieve their anxieties via the mother tongue. Developing a trusting relationship with parents and the local community is of vital importance if good home–school links are to be developed. Information about children's background and history can be an enormous help to schools in determining the provision to be made and in identifying any special educational needs.

Parents unfamiliar with the British education system may need to have structures and procedures explained. Many parents, keen to see their children get on at school, suppress the use of the child's first language at home and need to be encouraged to see its further development as an asset and not a stigma. A home-visiting programme can usefully extend the work possible in school, as can the provision of first language interpretation at parents' meetings or reviews. Bilingual assistants also have a key role to play in extending children's curriculum access through the use of mother tongue. Regular exposure to the child's first language can:

- aid concept development and hence second language acquisition;
- boost the child's confidence and self-esteem;
- allow the child to demonstrate proficiency and skill.

Finally, bilingual language assistants can help the school develop a multicultural and multilingual ethos through providing multilingual resources and exposing all the children to cultural diversity, e.g. via the teaching of dance, cookery or traditional crafts. Feedback to teachers can also ensure that school curricula and policies are anti-racist and free from possible cultural misunderstandings.

Parents in the classroom

The presence of parents in classrooms has been a reality in many schools since the Plowden Report (DES 1967) or even earlier. More recently, an HMI survey (DES 1991) reported that in all but two of the 32 primary schools visited, parents regularly helped in classrooms. Nevertheless, a variety of studies in the 1980s (e.g. Mortimore and Mortimore 1984) confirmed that only around 5 per cent of parents are actually involved on a regular basis. In their survey Cyster *et al.* (1979) found 65 per cent of parent helpers to be involved in sewing and minor repairs, while only 26 per cent heard children read. However, over time there has been a gradual move away from menial to more educational tasks.

Bastiani (1989) considers that parents volunteer to help in school for three reasons:

1. to help their own children,
2. to help the school, and
3. to meet their own needs.

Effective In-class Support

Schools should be aware of these factors in organising a programme of parental involvement and need to draw up a balance sheet of costs and benefits (Wolfendale 1992). Teachers vary widely in their attitude to parental involvement. Although some welcome the extra help, others are less than enthusiastic. Fears expressed by teachers interviewed by Cyster *et al.* (1979) were wide-ranging (see Figure 3.5).

Thomas (1992) groups these concerns under four main headings:

1. managerial objections: coping with extra adults in the classroom;
2. professional objections: parents may undermine professional skills of teachers and nursery nurses and put jobs at risk;
3. educational objections: teachers can do the job adequately without needing the help of parents;
4. personal objections: teachers may feel embarrassed and their authority compromised by the presence of parents.

In fact, less than one school in ten in the Cyster *et al.* survey, reported that their fears had been confirmed. Yet worries remain in a significant number of schools and many hard-pressed teachers still see the presence of parents in their classroom as an intrusion and an inconvenience.

With cuts in schools' budgets and the need for paid assistants to specialise in working with children with special needs, the more general support roles are falling increasingly on willing volunteers. Yet as the Professional Association of Teachers (McQuillan 1987)

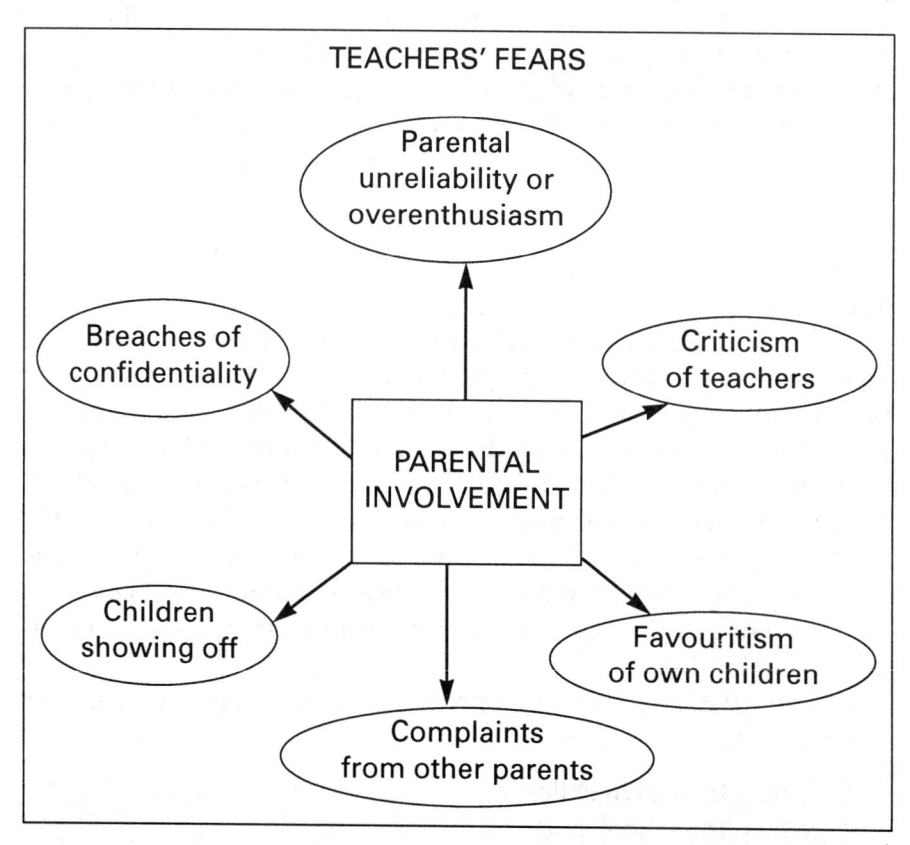

Figure 3.5

emphasises, no school should be stampeded into having parents in the classroom before they are ready. Setting objectives for parental involvement is essential if problems are to be avoided.

Without the support of their senior managers, some teachers may feel unable to meet the needs of those parents who see involvement in school as a way of overcoming feelings of inadequacy. Yet it may be just these parents and their children who would benefit most from successful involvement in school. The allocation of overall responsibility for parental involvement to one key member of staff can be of real value as can a policy on parental involvement developed by staff and parents together. Tizard *et al.* (1982) focus on effective communication between parents and teachers and the organisation of support as key factors in a successful partnership. Teachers need training in how to work with parents and ongoing help in resolving potential sources of conflict.

Guidelines for parent volunteers, spelling out the need for confidentiality and reliability, as well as the key responsibilities, can ease a lot of anxieties on both sides. One particularly useful booklet for schools (Humberside 1995) includes a summary of points to consider when planning to involve parents in the classroom (see Figure 3.6). By providing such guidance, schools can ensure that parents who volunteer do so understanding what is expected of them. There is now considerable evidence to show that the involvement of parents with their own children's learning can have beneficial results. However, this role should not be confused with that of parent volunteer. It is better, therefore, to avoid putting volunteers into classes containing their own children.

Basic information on the layout of the school, the organisation of the school day, school rules and the responsibilities of key staff should always be provided for new volunteers, as well as telling them where personal possessions can be left, arrangements for tea-making, lunchbreaks and emergency procedures. The best-organised schools have a short Volunteers' Handbook which is regularly updated and contains all relevant information, avoiding incessant questioning or inadvertent mistakes.

Some schools believe that the presence of parents in the staffroom prevents staff unwinding and talking about individual pupils. If that is the feeling, the provision of a separate parents' room may be a way forward. In other schools, parent volunteers are accepted as honorary members of staff and are trusted not to spread confidential information. However, each school needs to find its own solution, as unless all participants are comfortable the programme is likely to fail.

In taking on parent volunteers, schools should be clear whether they are prepared to accept all offers of help or whether they wish to be selective. While some schools fear the over-assertive parent or the one with poor social skills, there are real problems in turning down genuine offers of help. Far better is a judicious matching of individual volunteers to specific duties. Initially, it is better for new parent volunteers to be given straightforward tasks such as sharpening

MANAGING PARENTS IN THE CLASSROOM

Establish what skills the parents are offering
To be effective helpers need to feel confident. Don't assume that parents have the skills or training to cope with classroom situations

Ensure that the teacher remains in control
By law, parents should work under the direct supervision of the teacher, who should be constantly aware of what is happening in the group

Parents must be briefed and be clear what is expected of them
The teacher is responsible for the work the children do. She must explain how much help to give, how to question the children and what concepts are to be learnt

Parents need to feel valued
Teachers should never take parental help for granted. Without being patronising, give praise when praise is due

Groups must be kept small
Parents should not be expected to control large groups of children. Their main value is to work one-to-one or with small groups on specific well-designed tasks

Figure 3.6

pencils or tidying cupboards. Once they are comfortable in the classroom, responsibilities should be increased in line with the parent's expressed wishes and their particular skills.

Where they have specific strengths, these can be used to advantage, e.g. in preparing displays or taking groups for cookery or computer studies. Above all, parents should be made to feel wanted and valued by school staff. The problems experienced by many paid support staff are even more acute for volunteers. A formally-drawn-up policy for parental involvement, endorsed by the governors and supported by a programme of staff support and training, will go a long way to ensure that the input of parent volunteers is of a high standard and benefits the pupils, the staff and the parents themselves.

Chapter 4

Support at Secondary Level

> Working in classrooms puts support teachers in a unique position for both preventing and meeting special educational needs which no other situation provides. (Hart 1986)

The role of the support teacher

Research by Lee and Henkhuzens (1996) confirms the fact that in the secondary sector, support for students with SEN can be provided in a variety of different ways. Many schools still offer at least some individual or small group withdrawal. Nevertheless, the bulk of learning support is now provided in mainstream classrooms. Some of this in-class support is being provided by learning support assistants, however most secondary schools still prefer to use qualified teachers. When organised well, in-class support can smooth the way for subject teachers to deliver their lessons with minimal disruption, as well as improving the low self-esteem of students with special needs, encouraging them to move from dependence to independence (Welding 1996).

In some instances the SENCO performs this task on his or her own, or with additional input from an LEA support service; in others, the SENCO manages a team of support teachers and assistants. Some schools encourage subject staff to support each other, while yet others draw up a support timetable from the entire staff complement, timetabling those with free periods to support colleagues across the curriculum.

Unfortunately, as Garnett (1988) notes, too many schools set up a system of support before fully considering the implications of the chosen model. All too often senior management teams look purely at the quantity of support and devote little time to evaluating its quality. Questions that need to be addressed include:

- What type of support is required in any particular situation?
- Where is teaching, as opposed to ancillary, support required?
- Which staff are available to support colleagues?
- Do they have the requisite skills?

Effective In-class Support

- Do they view the role positively or is it seen as an imposition?
- How are the respective roles of subject and support teacher defined?

Garnett suggests that the role of the support teacher, working in the mainstream classroom, should have three major components (see Figure 4.1). To be effective, the support teacher needs to be able to:

- listen to and understand the concerns of colleagues;
- decide on priorities for intervention;
- anticipate the needs of colleagues and students;
- offer a range of strategies;
- grasp the essential components in most subject areas;
- be constructive and encouraging;
- know who to refer to for further advice;
- be flexible in negotiation.

THE ROLE OF THE SUPPORT TEACHER

General support
- Increasing the adult/child ratio
- Making the lesson accessible to all
- Identifying and supporting students needing extra help
- Managing difficult behaviour

Tutorial support
- Prompting and encouraging named students
- Teaching new skills
- Counselling
- Pre-teaching content of next lesson
- Reinforcing work already covered

SECONDARY SUPPORT TEACHER

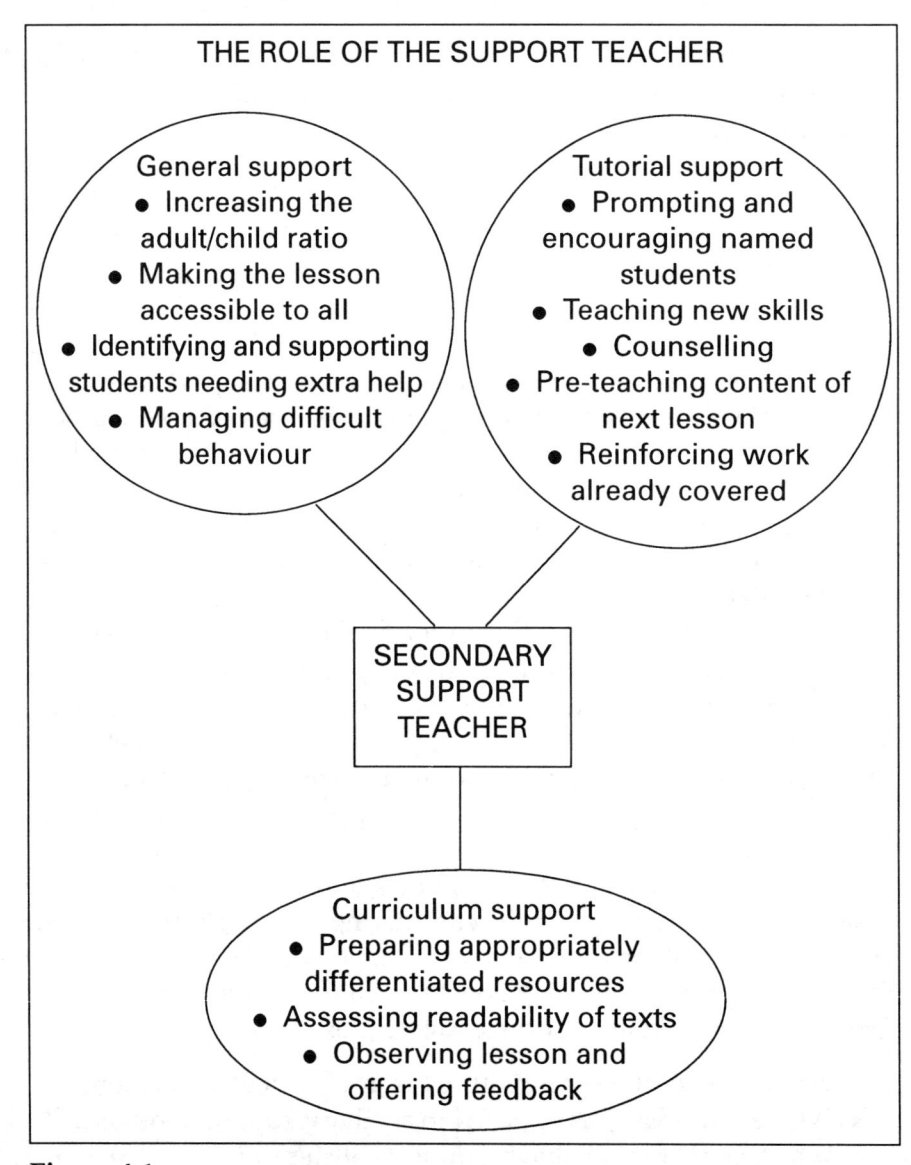

Curriculum support
- Preparing appropriately differentiated resources
- Assessing readability of texts
- Observing lesson and offering feedback

Figure 4.1

Unfortunately, in some settings, problems arise. Bearn and Smith (1998) note the large gap between the ideal role of the support teacher and the actual role in practice. Subject teachers in their study perceived the role of support staff as that of a general dogsbody or a classroom assistant, while support teachers talked of feeling disempowered by having to relinquish authority, even when supporting in their own subject area. Hart (1986) comments on situations where the presence of a support teacher encourages subject staff to ignore the needs of pupils with SEN, considering them to be the sole responsibility of the support teacher. Rather than leading to improvements in classroom approaches, the provision of in-class support can reinforce bad practice and let subject teachers off the hook.

Other unhelpful practices are described by Best (1991) who talks about the support teacher as:

- the servant of the class teacher, carrying out the teacher's instructions without question;
- the servant of the child, responding immediately to the named child who has a problem;
- another pupil, trying desperately to find out what the lesson is about;
- translator, trying to paper over the cracks of a poorly differentiated curriculum;
- foreman, policing the class to ensure that students complete their work, however inappropriate.

Exactly the same issues are highlighted in studies of the role of the language support teacher, supporting students from ethnic minorities (Williamson 1989). Without a whole-school consensus on the purpose of support and the way in which support staff should be deployed, practice will be developed on an *ad hoc* basis. Lovey (1996), in her study of support in the secondary school, reported that most of the support teachers she interviewed talked of frustration in working with teachers who were not clear about their role. 'Some found themselves sharpening the pencils and sitting in silence during long periods of lessons, while the child they were supposed to be supporting struggled to understand the lesson'.

In such situations, as Margerison (1997) comments, schools might be better withdrawing support or replacing a support teacher with a classroom assistant. To be effective, support teachers need to develop a range of consultancy skills over and above those they require as effective teachers. Morris and Parker (1997) consider that the most important are:

- sensitivity, to overcome the defensiveness of the insecure teacher;
- realism, to accept that certain practices cannot be changed;
- communication skills, to develop a two-way dialogue with the subject teacher without being seen to challenge or intimidate, and
- observation skills, to enable them to determine the help required by individual students in different settings.

Subject teachers also have a part to play in establishing a positive support climate in their classroom. Firstly, it is essential that they value their colleague and appreciate the contribution they are able to make. This should be conveyed to the students to avoid comments such as 'He's not a proper teacher', reported by Margerison (1997). They need to put aside sufficient time to brief the support teacher about the content of the lesson and its aims and then should stick to the agreed plan (Best 1991). They also need to share their basic philosophy to ensure that students are not presented with conflicting instructions.

One highly effective way of raising the awareness of teaching staff to the needs of support workers, is to insist that all teachers who are supported by others also work in a support role themselves. After experiencing some of the frustrations at first hand, they are likely to acquire a greater sympathy with those who support them.

Teaching in partnership

Putting an extra teacher into the classroom 'in the hope that the combined efforts of two people will solve the problem or keep the lid on the behaviour' (Margerison 1997) has, in recent years, been the most common response to special needs issues. Many schools have responded in much the same way to the challenges of second language learners.

However, without careful planning and ongoing monitoring, the arrangements made can fail to meet the needs of the subject teacher, the support teacher or, more frequently, the students. Efforts can be duplicated and two teachers, rather than supporting each other, can get in each other's way (Thomas and Jackson 1986) or unwittingly undermine each other. A culture of dependency can be set up, whereby students rely on adult help being available as soon as a problem is identified and fail to develop problem-solving strategies of their own.

Studies on the effectiveness of cooperative teaching (e.g. Allan 1995) suggest that in too many instances there is little evidence of professional collaboration or involvement of support teachers in discussions about the curriculum or about appropriate teaching approaches. Work in one school (Bearn and Smith 1998) highlights some of the belief systems held by subject teachers which are likely to prevent the development of collaborative working. These include the view that:

- there are 'special' needs that are outside their teaching range and should be dealt with by specialists;
- there are territorial boundaries and issues of ownership involved in 'sharing' classes with support teachers, even when in-class support has been long established;
- staff who elected and trained to teach pupils with SEN are better equipped and therefore more responsible for teaching them;

- within a whole-class setting, the needs of the many are greater than the needs of the few.

To overcome potential difficulties, it is essential that a whole-school approach is adopted. The development of Partnership Teaching (Bourne and McPake 1991) used predominantly with second language learners, ensures that groups of staff work together in developing appropriate curricula for all pupils (see Figure 4.2), rather than relying on *ad hoc* input from a support teacher in the classroom. In this way, teachers can create conditions in which all students can optimise their learning as well as developing their thinking, study skills, personal organisation and social relationships (Quah and Jones 1997).

THE PARTNERSHIP CYCLE

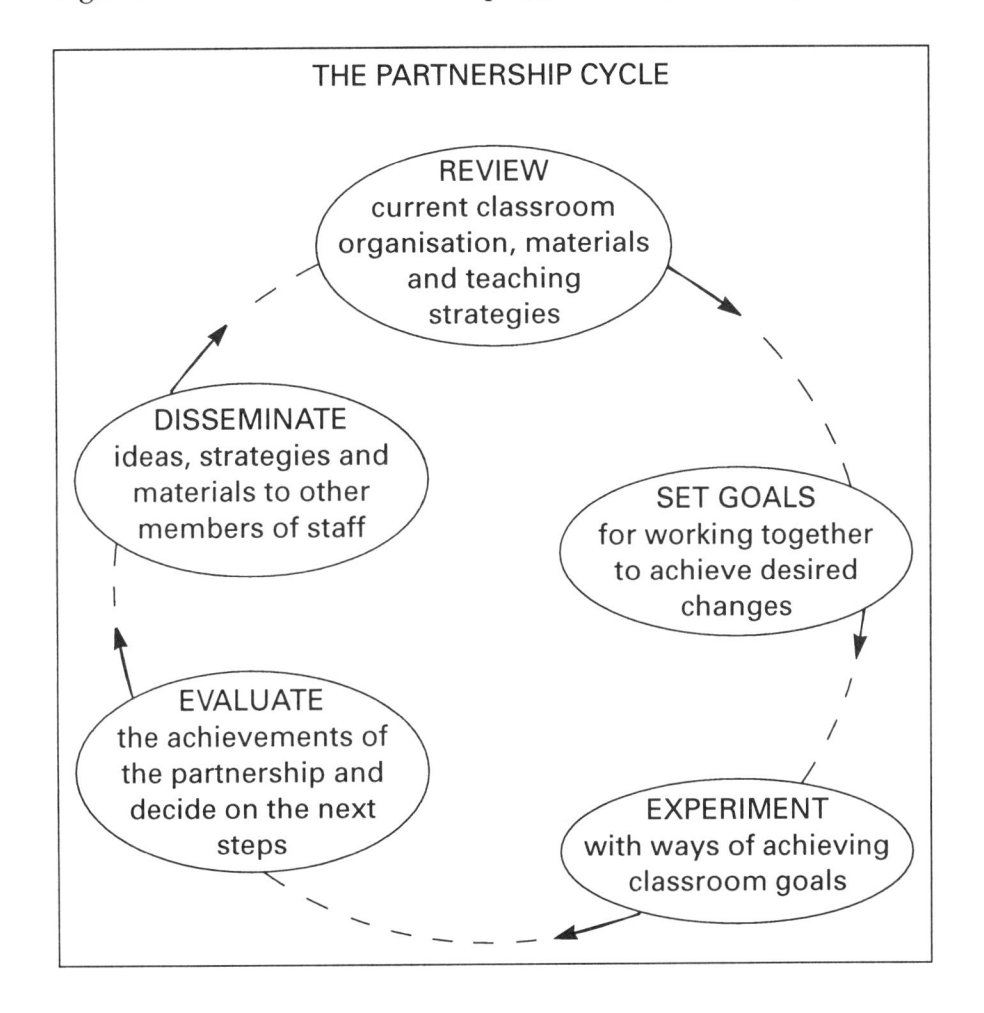

- REVIEW current classroom organisation, materials and teaching strategies
- SET GOALS for working together to achieve desired changes
- EXPERIMENT with ways of achieving classroom goals
- EVALUATE the achievements of the partnership and decide on the next steps
- DISSEMINATE ideas, strategies and materials to other members of staff

Figure 4.2

We were learning from each other and trying to help each other in the classroom situation. It wasn't just the children learning – it was us as teachers learning at the same time (teacher quoted in Bourne and McPake 1991).

Two teachers working in partnership, can use the opportunities presented by more flexible working practices, to encourage students to analyse problem situations and negotiate the support they need. They can facilitate peer support and model techniques to increase pupils' self-management, instead of responding directly to specific difficulties. Nevertheless, as Ireson (1992) remarks, collaboration takes time and relies on agreeing aims, goals and sequences of teaching. Both adults need to negotiate their respective roles and responsibilities. These will vary from one partnership to another depending on the respective skills of the two partners.

Collaborative patterns of working can be established equally well between two teachers with subject-specific expertise or between a subject specialist and a special needs or a specialist language teacher. Jordan (1994) describes a process she terms 'collaborative classroom consultation' where the support teacher has three goals:

1. to solve immediate problems about the learning situation defined by a colleague;
2. to assist the colleague to master skills and knowledge to deal with a similar problem in the future;
3. to ultimately change the way in which this colleague works.

In developing this relationship, the two partners require:

- an acceptance and valuing of each other's skills;
- a shared understanding of the particular needs of individual students;
- a sharing of the aims of the curriculum and how these can be achieved;
- joint planning of teaching goals;
- joint preparation of resources;
- regular informal feedback;
- a shared framework for more formal monitoring and evaluation.

To achieve these aims, the partners should ask themselves the following questions (Garnett 1988):

- How can we find the time to liaise?
- How often do we need to meet?
- How can we support each other in planning and preparation?
- What resources do we need?
- Who will prepare what?
- Do we need a joint recording system?
- How will we manage class discipline?
- How will we evaluate our joint effectiveness?

In looking at the development of inclusive classrooms, Ainscow (1995) gives powerful support to the wider use of teamwork as a way of encouraging innovation and experimentation. Without the support of colleagues, teachers are more likely to support pupils within existing structures or to carry out relatively minor modifications of their teaching approaches. However, teachers working in partnership can use dialogue to stimulate critical reflection and support each other in improvisation and the evaluation of new methodologies. As Fullan

(1992) comments 'Teachers need to converse about teaching and learning in order to improve'.

Peer coaching can be a highly effective way of developing knowledge and increasing teachers' repertoire of effective instructional practice. As Swafford (1998) notes, in-class coaching can take several forms depending on its purpose and goals.

- Technical coaching involves transfer to the classroom of teaching methods introduced via a workshop or training course. Here two or more teachers work together to introduce new approaches.
- Expert coaching utilises specially trained teachers, with a particular expertise they wish to pass on to colleagues via modelling, observation and feedback.
- Reciprocal coaching allows pairs of teachers to observe and coach each other, to improve practice across a subject department or the whole school.
- Reflective and cognitive coaching involve engaging teachers in an on-going dialogue about their classroom practice.

As Kovic (1996) observes: 'Peer coaching can help build a professional culture that supports teachers who are knowledgeable and responsive to students, regardless of their needs'.

Working with support assistants

The majority of secondary schools still rely heavily on qualified teachers to provide support for students with SEN. However, with the advent of the SEN Code of Practice (DfEE 1994a), learning support assistants are becoming an increasingly cost-effective addition to the support team. Cheminais (1997) notes that in her school, she was able to employ four support assistants for the price of one teacher with an 'A' allowance.

In some respects, providing effective LSA support in the secondary school is easier than in the primary sector. Most year groups contain several children with SEN and, as a consequence, support can be deployed more flexibly to support a variety of children in different ways. Funding in the secondary sector is more generous and therefore most schools are in a position, if they so choose, to enhance the number of support assistant hours provided by the LEA via statements. Learning support assistants in the same school can support each other (Macaulay 1998) and can take on the induction of newly appointed staff, without the need to call on outside agencies or link with other schools.

On the other hand, there are particular problems rarely encountered in primary schools. The open-plan primary classroom inhabited by a range of different adults is now commonplace. However, many secondary teachers are still most comfortable when they can close the door on their classroom and be left to teach their own classes. The presence of another adult can be perceived as a threat or a 'spy in the classroom' (Balshaw 1991).

LSAs may find the content of lessons difficult to comprehend and may feel no better prepared than the students themselves. This is particularly true when an individual assistant is expected to support students across the whole curriculum. Increasingly in the secondary sector, support assistants are being attached to particular departments or faculties. This has several advantages.

Support assistants in a single faculty:

- have fewer staff to liaise with each week;
- can work in areas where they feel most comfortable;
- can develop curriculum knowledge;
- can attend departmental meetings.

Subject teachers:

- can get to know their departmental assistants very well;
- can ensure that their assistants understand the particular demands of their curriculum area;
- have the opportunity to develop common working practices;
- can hand over routine tasks, e.g. setting up the lab or reorganising the furniture for discussion groups.

Students:

- can be sure that the assistant understands the subject content;
- can be allowed independence between classes, instead of being minded by a personal assistant;
- can avoid becoming overdependent on one person by learning to seek support from a number of sources;
- are more likely to be handled consistently by the teacher and the assistant in any one subject area, assuming that there is effective communication between the staff involved.

LSAs working with the same teacher soon learn what is expected of them and of the pupils. Where assistants are expected to support a whole range of teachers, each with his or her own personal way of running the class, consistency is much harder to achieve. As a result, assistants and teachers may unwittingly find themselves undermining each other. It is therefore imperative in the secondary school that effective communication systems are established.

While time is at a premium in all schools, most regular partners can snatch the odd moment between activities to exchange ideas or give feedback. Support assistants who have to move with the students when the bell rings have no time to talk to teachers before or after the lesson. Many complain that they have no idea what work is going to be covered in the lesson and so they are running hard to keep up the whole time, to the detriment of the pupils. Dedicated planning time is essential if support is to be effective. Communication needs to exist at several levels:

(a) At the whole school level:

- Access to information routinely offered to teachers via daily briefings, staff meetings, etc.
- Regular meetings with the SENCO or a deputy.

(b) At the departmental level:

- Up-to-date information on curriculum issues.
- Opportunities to familiarise themselves with teaching materials and equipment before they are used with students.
- Information about the layout of subject areas and knowledge about how to access resources.

(c) At the classroom level:

- Knowledge of how individual teachers run their lessons and the type of support required.
- How each teacher wishes them to deal with issues of discipline.
- How to respond to requests for help, visits to the toilet or accessing resources such as pencils and rubbers.
- Regular opportunities to give feedback to the teacher.

(d) At the individual child level:

- Information about the nature of the child's difficulties and the provision laid down in the statement.
- Which external support services are involved with the child.
- Opportunities to discuss the child with the SENCO, outside agencies and, where appropriate, the parents.

Despite the difficulties, most secondary teachers who have worked with LSAs value their presence (Cheminais 1997). Similarly, for the most part, the students being supported appreciate the help they are given (Lee and Henkhuzens 1996). In their study, LSAs were generally seen as supporting the whole class rather than targeted individuals and this was preferred by the students, who generally disliked being singled out. Within the classroom, secondary LSAs perform a similar range of duties to those carried out in primary schools, although with a greater emphasis on literacy-related activities (see Figure 4.3).

As one LSA, reported by Cheminais (1997) commented:

> There is certainly more to the job than just sharpening pencils, wiping noses and listening to children read. Yes, I do these tasks on a few occasions, but my daily work is far more challenging, complex and exhausting. Imagine how it feels to support SEN

THE SECONDARY SUPPORT ASSISTANT

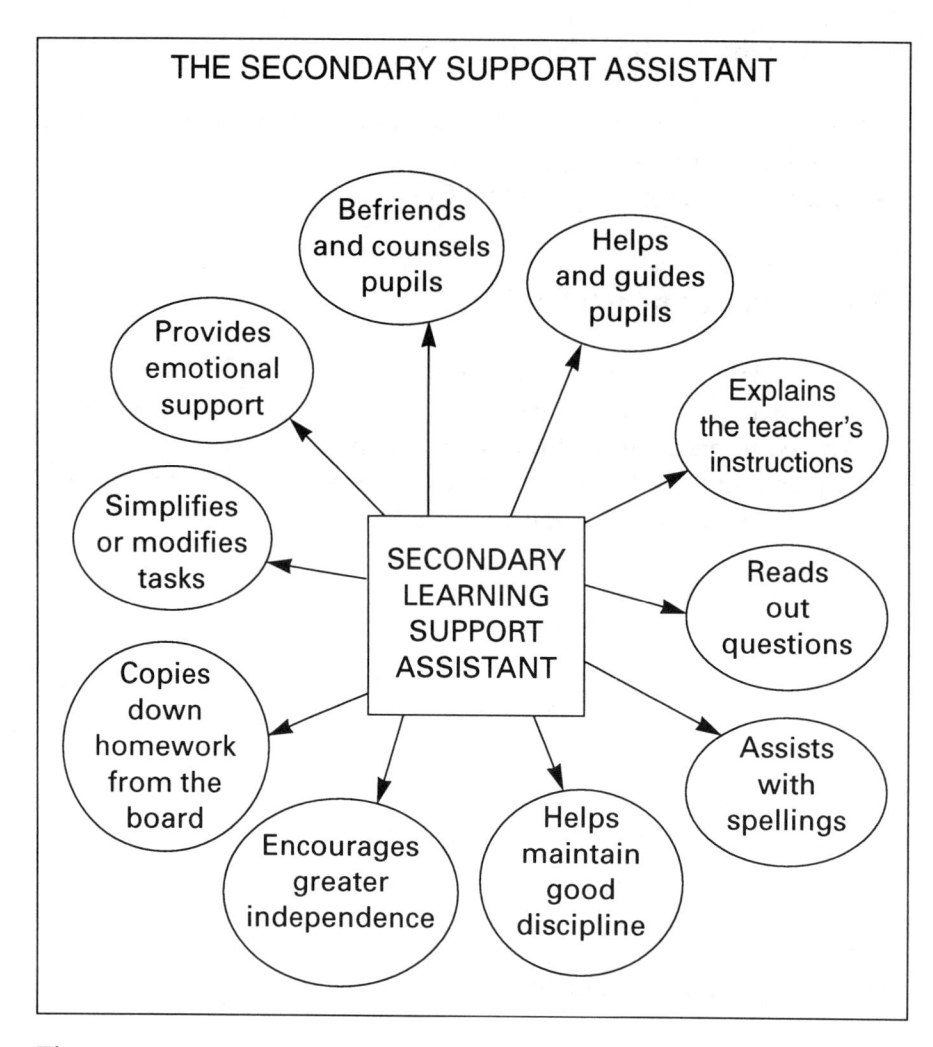

- Befriends and counsels pupils
- Helps and guides pupils
- Provides emotional support
- Explains the teacher's instructions
- Simplifies or modifies tasks
- SECONDARY LEARNING SUPPORT ASSISTANT
- Reads out questions
- Copies down homework from the board
- Assists with spellings
- Encourages greater independence
- Helps maintain good discipline

Figure 4.3

pupils in nine different areas and to work with up to twelve different subject teachers each week.

Developing a support timetable

The task of setting up a support timetable in a large secondary school is both complex and problematic if not carried out with adequate consultation. Subject teachers may be press-ganged into providing cross-curricular support in their free periods, with neither the subject expertise nor the specialist skills required to support pupils with particular needs. Unwilling conscripts are unlikely to prioritise the support role and will devote neither the time nor the energy to making it work.

Teachers may be used where an unqualified assistant would be equally effective, and a far better use of scarce resources. On the other hand, an assistant may be used when the presence of a qualified teacher could have lead to a far higher level of analysis, consultancy and joint planning, to the benefit of all the students. Support may be targeted at individual students when the real need is to support subject teachers, helping improve their curriculum differentiation or mode of delivery. Support may be provided in lessons where the class teacher is well able to meet the needs of the students unaided or is unwilling to cooperate with a support worker. Conversely, teachers who can cope alone may be denied in-class support, even where such provision would be used to the benefit of teacher and students alike.

Prior to the start of the new school year, the SENCO and those responsible for timetabling, should carry out a whole-school audit which aims to assess:

- the needs of individuals and groups of students;
- the needs of individual teachers and subject departments;
- the staff available to perform a support role;
- the skills and attitudes of these staff.

In reviewing the needs of individual students, schools need to be clear about the aims of support. In some situations, this is best provided by a classroom assistant who is able to befriend and encourage. In others, the needs of individual students require particular expertise in the acquisition of literacy skills, the use of specialised equipment or the management of particularly challenging behaviour. Students who sign or who have very limited understanding of English may need access to a teacher or an assistant with particular language skills. Blind students may need support from someone familiar with Braille.

For some students, subject-focused support in particular areas of the curriculum is most appropriate. For others, an integrated cross-curricular approach (Copeland 1990) is more helpful. Some students learn most effectively in a class taught by two subject specialists working in partnership. This approach is particularly effective with pupils who find it difficult to accept the need for support and resent individual attention. Others welcome a more personalised approach from someone who has a deeper understanding of their difficulties.

The grouping of pupils can have a major bearing on the way in which support is organised. Although some students feel comfortable working alongside others with similar difficulties, such groupings can exacerbate behavioural problems, as students have fewer good role-models and may feel stigmatised. On the other hand, it may not be possible to spread support across a whole series of mixed-ability classes. Thus the most cost-effective approach might be to pair up students with similar needs or target particular classes for support.

In reviewing the support needs of teachers, Morris and Parker (1997) advocate the use of departmental SEN reviews, focusing on four or five mutually-agreed objectives. Such reviews can identify the support needs of individual teachers or of subject departments. They can also help teachers articulate both the level and type of support that best meets their identified needs. At the same time, effective review can inspire confidence and improve morale. Following review, schools should come up with their own unique model of support rather than adopting someone else's.

Thus in one school, reported by Pickup (1995), all departments decided that they wanted either the time to do their own support or an allocation of time from a support teacher with an appropriate subject specialism. In another, described by Wheal (1995), five staff were given cross-curricular responsibility for SEN as a team. They worked with subject departments and with individual teachers, helping the development of more effective teaching styles and strategies. Here support teachers saw their key role as supporting staff development.

In many schools, the more traditional model, described by Bearn and Smith (1998) is still the norm. Here, support is essentially child-focused with support teachers or assistants taking on the key responsibility for meeting the learning needs of identified students (Dyer 1988). While the involvement of the subject teacher can vary, from a true collaboration to a total abrogation of responsibility for the student's learning, support is perceived purely as a way of meeting the needs of pupils, not those of teachers or of the school as a whole. Where this model works well, teachers are clear about the aims of support, support staff have clearly-defined job descriptions and the students themselves have been involved in negotiating the type of support to be offered.

In all schools, arrangements should be in place to ensure that priority support needs are met when staff are absent, for example through illness or for training. Regrettably, this occurs all too infrequently and as Bearn (personal communication) comments, supply teachers are rarely if ever timetabled in a support role. Nevertheless, for many students with significant needs, unreliable and unpredictable support is worse than no support at all. To avoid distress, an understudy is required when their support teacher or assistant is unavailable. For others, however, support is desirable but by no means essential. In these instances, the loss of support, on occasions, will have no serious knock-on effects.

To avoid uncertainty for staff and students, some schools provide support teachers and assistants with detailed timetables containing backup activities and cover procedures (see Figure 4.4). These suggest alternative tasks to carry out when the student they are supporting is absent, or the subject teacher feels that support is not required in a particular lesson. At the same time, it alerts them to when they might be called on to cover for an absent colleague.

As long as subject teachers and students are aware that the support teacher or assistant might be withdrawn at times, this should not present problems, as long as both the students and the teacher are informed in good time. On the other hand, the use of support staff for general staff cover, or other duties unrelated to SEN, is not to be recommended other than in an emergency. Schools who see support as a low priority in the general scheme of things, cannot avoid conveying negative messages about the value placed on students with SEN.

SUPPORT TIMETABLE: Anne Schofield Autumn Term 1998

PERIOD		MONDAY	TUESDAY	WEDNESDAY	THURSDAY	FRIDAY
1.	9.15–9.55	Maths. Room 3. Mr James. 3G. Support Sally and Ben. General class support.	Subject. Room. Teacher. Class. Particular duties. Backup duties.			
2.	9.55–10.35	History. Room 17. Mrs Sanders. 2E. Support Brian. (Backup: photocopy, file, prepare worksheets, etc.)				
BREAK	10.35–10.55	Check John's hearing aids.				
3.	10.55–11.05	Tea break.				
	11.05–11.35	English. Room 8. Mr Francis. 1S. General group work.				
4.	11.35–12.15	French. Language lab. 1. Miss Graham. 3M. Support Jenny. (Backup: support Mr Smith 4H. German. Lang lab. 2.)				
DINNER TIME		Spelling club. Room 6.				
5.	1.30–2.10	Science. Physics lab. Mrs Porter. 1S. Work with groups. (May need to cover for LSA absences instead.)				
6.	2.10–2.50	Science (as period 5). Help least able pupils record ideas on paper. (May need to cover for LSA absences.)				
7.	2.50–3.15	Medical room. Sam. Delivery of individual therapy programme. (Phone calls, etc. if away)				
	3.15–3.30	Meeting with SENCO.				

Figure 4.4

Chapter 5

Support in the Special School

In the majority of classrooms within the mainstream sector, class teachers take sole responsibility for their pupils for much of the time. On the other hand, this situation is rare in most special schools. Although partnership teaching is uncommon, except during periods of appraisal or innovation (Newman and Rose 1990), most special school teachers are supported by at least one additional adult for most of the working week. In some cases these adults will be qualified nursery nurses or classroom assistants with additional training. However, they may equally be unqualified care assistants or volunteers. In such instances, as Mason (1978) points out, it is the head's responsibility to make sure that they are given sufficient training to enable them to do their job effectively.

In comparing the role of the support assistant in the special school with that of their counterpart in the mainstream, certain significant differences need to be taken into consideration.

1. Most SSAs are full-time and on permanent contracts. Many have worked in the same school for many years and know both the staff and the pupils extremely well. In a survey of 27 ancillary staff in seven special schools, Woolf and Bassett (1988) found the average length of service in the same school was 7¼ years, with 37 per cent having served for over 10 years.
2. SSAs are usually members of a sizeable group of staff working in a similar way. They are therefore able to share problems and support each other. For example, Julia Voisey, a nursery nurse spotlighted by Peter (1993) worked with six other teaching assistants in a school for 42 pupils with language and communication difficulties. Similarly, in Millwood School, a special school for 86 primary-aged pupils with learning difficulties in Bury, there are 11 full-time and two part-time support assistants (Emblem, personal communication).
3. SSAs, although normally attached to one class for most of their time, would be expected to support all the pupils, not just one

The role of the special school assistant (SSA)

Effective In-class Support

individual or a particular small group. Woolf and Bassett (1988) in their survey of seven special schools, found 81 per cent of classroom assistants were based in one class with the same teacher throughout most of their working week. However, none had responsibility for individual pupils. At Millwood School, teaching assistants are given a job description (see Figure 5.1) in which their two main duties are:

- to assist the teaching staff with a class of children, and
- to encourage the development of all pupils.

4. Teachers in a special school have chosen to work with pupils with SEN. They are, therefore, less likely than their mainstream colleagues to delegate full teaching responsibilities to an SSA. Nevertheless as Emblem (personal communication) comments: 'SSAs are still at the whim of the teacher they work with. Whatever the philosophy of the school, within a classroom the teacher still has a great deal of freedom and the SSA little by right.'

Historically, the role of the welfare assistant in the special school was one of care and of attention to the children's social needs. Nevertheless, those interviewed by Woolf and Bassett (1988) were already spending around 75 per cent of their time on educational tasks. Even though the tasks performed by teachers and support assistants may be similar, there is a clear distinction between the two roles in terms of responsibility and decision-making.

Despite this, as Turner (1985) points out, 'The increase in the number of ancillary staff in special schools heightens the possibility of conflict and may create many new and delicate role-definition problems for the head'. In Woolf and Bassett's survey, nearly all the assistants questioned said they were able to talk to their teacher about their job and how they were used. However, only 30 per cent had a written job description.

On average, 64 per cent of a teaching assistant's time at Millwood School is spent under the direct supervision of the teacher, 16 per cent alone but within a teacher-designated framework and 20 per cent independently. Within the classroom, 80 per cent of the time is spent supervising children's activities and 13 per cent reading stories or leading singing games. Of the time spent outside the classroom, 20 per cent is spent teaching children individually or in small groups and 40 per cent supervising individuals around the school or on outside visits.

Despite some significant differences in role, many of the issues raised by support assistants in the special school sector mirror those expressed by their colleagues in the mainstream. Assistants in both settings express concern about the absence of a career structure and the limited opportunities for training. Out of a sample of 27 assistants interviewed by Woolf and Bassett (1988) the following responses were recorded:

MILLWOOD SCHOOL JOB DESCRIPTION NNEB

JOB TITLE
Teaching Assistant
Salary Scale: APT Scale Grades 7–15

RESPONSIBLE TO
The head teacher

DUTIES

1. Pupils
(a) To assist the teaching staff in offering a broad, balanced, relevant and differentiated curriculum to a class of children with a wide range of learning difficulties and associated disabilities.
(b) To encourage the social, emotional, physical and intellectual development of all pupils.

2. Adults
To work in partnership with parents, carers and colleagues.

3. School development
To play an active part in the development of the school by being a member of working groups set up from time to time to review curriculum, organisation, or other functions of the school.

4. Personal and professional development
To maintain and increase relevant knowledge and skills through professional development activities.

5. Resources
To assist teaching staff in maintaining and organising classroom equipment.

6. Other duties
To undertake any duties of an equal nature appropriate to the post.

CONDITIONS OF EMPLOYMENT
The conditions of employment outlined in the Conditions of Service of the National Joint Council for Local Authorities' Administrative, Professional, Technical and Clerical Services apply.

REVIEW
This Job Description will be reviewed at least once a year, in consultation with the postholder.

Figure 5.1

- Only 59 per cent had attended an in-service course of some sort in the previous year, although all but one said they would welcome the opportunity for further training.
- Only 70 per cent were invited to attend staff meetings, although 89 per cent said they would like to do so.
- Just over half took part in parents' consultation meetings but only 30 per cent had a meeting with their teacher at the start of each day. Of those that did not, most said that it would be useful.

Training opportunities, however, vary significantly from one school to another. Peter (1993) notes that Julia Voisey and her colleagues are able to attend four or five in-service courses a year, organised by the school. At Millwood, support staff attend the school's five LEA Professional Activity Days and are encouraged to take part in the Bury Certificate for Special Support Assistants, alongside colleagues from mainstream schools. Nevertheless, staff are generally expected to attend training sessions in their own time without additional pay, funding is limited and few courses address special-school-related issues specifically.

Despite the problems, most support assistants in special schools enjoy their work and feel valued members of staff. Almost all of the 27 assistants questioned by Woolf and Bassett (1988) felt that they were respected by teaching colleagues. As Casteel (1985) comments: 'Ancillary staff in special schools . . . tend to give the lie to the adage that you get what you pay for. Their quality far exceeds their monetary reward'.

Therapy in the classroom

Prior to the establishment of a National Curriculum for all pupils, the work of therapists in the special school was largely separate from that of the teachers and their support assistants. Using the medical 'treatment' model, students were withdrawn for focused intervention on a 1:1 basis with a qualified therapist. However, in recent years it has become increasingly obvious that such an approach is not the one best suited to meet the needs of most pupils with disabilities. Further, budget restrictions have reduced the availability of qualified staff and rendered it essential that skills be shared across disciplines.

As Taylor *et al.* (1993) note, a withdrawal model has many disadvantages both for the therapist and for the pupil.

- Pupils often resent being taken away from normal activities and became difficult.
- Uncooperative pupils are less likely to benefit from targeted programmes and so the time may be wasted.
- Skills acquired in a withdrawal session are not often generalised back into the classroom.
- Teaching staff who have had no involvement in the therapy programme will find it difficult to reinforce the work being done by the therapist.

Teachers in schools for children with physical disabilities have in the past expressed concern about the disruption to children's educational programmes caused by visits to the physiotherapy room, planned to meet the needs of the therapist rather than the teacher. By incorporating therapy needs into the school curriculum, McQueen and McLellan (1994) found interruptions to lessons were virtually eliminated and pupils avoided missing enjoyable classroom-based activities or key aspects of school work.

Research by Cole *et al.* (1989) compared the outcomes of classroom-based and withdrawal physiotherapy. They found no significant differences in physical outcome measures. However, questionnaire responses indicated a strong preference of school staff for integrated approaches as 'therapy services facilitated academic work and led to a greater understanding of the aims and roles of therapists'. Similarly, research carried out by McQueen and McLellan (1996) found that not only did all staff participating in integrated models prefer such a regime but, by working alongside other professionals, they were able to explore jointly different ways of approaching the physical, learning and communication difficulties experienced by their pupils.

In the field of speech and language therapy, Stevens and Roulstone (1991) note that 'it is now widely acknowledged that intervention for speech and language problems should be a collaborative affair between all those involved with the child'. In their view, the role of the therapist will depend equally on the child's individual difficulties and on the approaches used by the class teacher. As Miller (1996) comments: 'A child's language needs to be viewed in terms of other people's behaviour and what is expected. In school it is necessary to take account, not only of how a child communicates but of how other people use language'. This information is best gathered collaboratively.

Nevertheless, some special school teachers still feel that therapy is an interruption to their teaching and are reluctant to let therapists into their classroom. To be most effective (Rossington, personal communication), the therapist needs to work with the teacher, slowly building confidence and sharing ideas. No professional likes to be told how to do their job and so therapists need to be sensitive to the feelings of teachers, particularly those used to 'traditional' ways of working.

In moving out of the medical room and into the classroom, the therapist gains access to a far wider range of information than before. By observing the child in normal interactions with adults and peers it is possible for the therapist to determine the level of their communicative ability and the problems they face in both individual and group interactions. As Taylor *et al.* (1993) note, classroom interactions offer exposure to a wide range of language roles. Working in the classroom, the therapist can contribute to the child's performance across the curriculum. Relevant models of communication can be demonstrated and both teachers and support staff encouraged to develop good practice that can be continued in the absence of the therapist. Interventions can focus on a range of skills (see Figure 5.2).

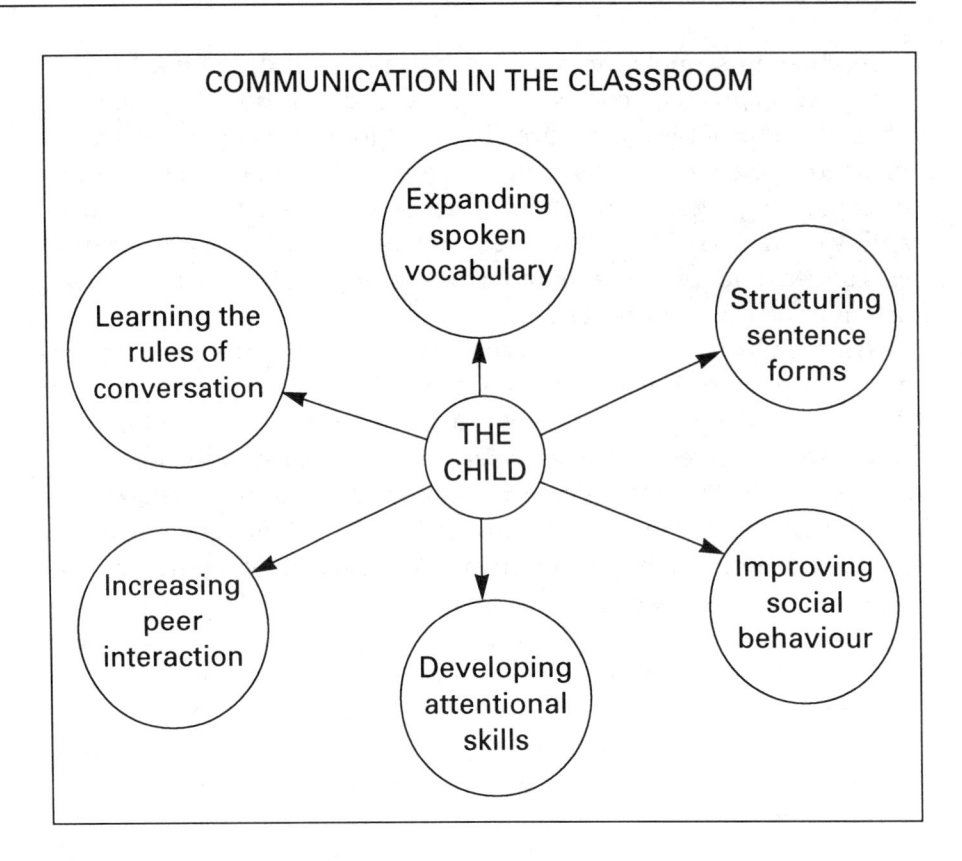

```
                COMMUNICATION IN THE CLASSROOM

                         ┌───────────┐
                         │ Expanding │
                         │  spoken   │
                         │vocabulary │
        ┌───────────┐    └───────────┘    ┌───────────┐
        │Learning the│          ↑          │ Structuring│
        │  rules of  │          │          │  sentence  │
        │conversation│          │          │   forms    │
        └───────────┘     ┌─────────┐     └───────────┘
              ↖           │   THE   │          ↗
                ←─────────│  CHILD  │─────────→
              ↙           └─────────┘          ↘
        ┌───────────┐          │          ┌───────────┐
        │ Increasing│          │          │ Improving │
        │    peer   │          ↓          │   social  │
        │interaction│    ┌───────────┐    │ behaviour │
        └───────────┘    │Developing │    └───────────┘
                         │attentional│
                         │   skills  │
                         └───────────┘
```

Figure 5.2

To develop collaborative practices Taylor *et al.* (1993) stress the need for:

- information sharing;
- establishing a shared understanding of the child's difficulties;
- establishing joint practices;
- joint assessment and goal setting;
- individual programme planning;
- developing an appropriate communication environment;
- joint evaluation and review.

Such joint practices, as Wright and Graham (1997) note, have benefits for both the child and the professionals. A holistic approach to the child is likely to result in greater innovation and hence an increased chance of productive interventions being devised. Similarly, sharing concerns with colleagues can provide personal and professional support both for teachers and therapists and lead to a reduction in stress. Writers such as Mackey and McQueen (1998) have begun to talk about 'integrated therapy' where the different therapies are not only delivered in an integrated way but are also integrated into the daily functional life of the child and family. This approach ensures that therapies are blended with the child's normal activities rather than being compartmentalised.

They advocate a move by professionals away from multidisciplinary approaches whereby interventions, although coordinated, remain separate, via interdisciplinary methods with partial collaboration between professionals, towards a transdisciplinary model. Here the different disciplines are integrated to provide a unified approach. Giangreco *et al.* (1989) talk of role release where common methods are used by team members from a range of disciplines. The outcomes, occurring in daily situations, are more meaningful and are naturally reinforced, increasing the educational relevance of therapy services.

This view is developed even further by those committed to conductive education. To ensure the delivery of a holistic programme, the separate roles of teacher, physiotherapist, speech therapist and psychologist are combined into that of the 'conductor' (Kozma 1995). While the underlying philosophy and methodology of conductive education may be questioned, the concept of joint training and true collaboration of professionals deserves serious thought.

Developing multi-disciplinary teams

For the majority of pupils in special schools, 'access to and progression through the National Curriculum is both an entitlement and a challenge' (NCC 1993). As teachers pointed out when the National Curriculum was introduced, it provides only part of the curriculum for pupils with exceptionally severe difficulties or with additional needs, for whom the opportunity to develop basic physical, perceptual, social and communication skills is at least of equal importance.

These skills can only be developed by allowing the child access to additional input from speech therapists, occupational therapists or physiotherapists and to programmes developed by staff skilled in a range of techniques such as counselling, educational therapy (Burridge 1995), mobility training or the development of independence. For some students, time must be found for the teaching of specific skills such as the use of BSL or Braille. For others, the use of relaxation (Sydney 1993), multisensory stimulation (Hirstwood 1994) or music therapy (Hill 1997) is considered crucial. Getting the balance right between these more traditional special school activities and the requirements of the National Curriculum is an ongoing issue for all staff working in the special school sector.

Sebba (1992), discussing the development of the National Curriculum for pupils in special schools, stressed that the guidance produced by the National Curriculum Council was aimed at all staff, not just teachers. In the same vein, the Schools Curriculum and Assessment Authority (SCAA 1996) talks about a range of professionals, including therapists and specialist support teachers, working as a team with teachers and parents, to meet the curricular needs of pupils with profound and multiple learning difficulties.

This collaborative approach is becoming increasingly important as the population of children in special schools changes. The establishment of integration policies in some LEAs, following the 1981 Education Act, has lead to the movement of the most able pupils from special schools into the mainstream. More recently, pressure from parents and professionals towards a greater degree of inclusion, reinforced by policy documents such as the recent Green Paper *Excellence for All Children* (DfEE 1997a), has meant that, increasingly, only pupils with the greatest level of need are now being placed in the special school sector.

Male (1996a), in a study of 75 schools for pupils with Moderate Learning Difficulties (MLD), found 92 per cent reporting a change in the needs of their pupils in recent years. 73 per cent reported more pupils with significant emotional and behavioural problems, 38 per cent reported more pupils with severe and complex needs, 15 per cent mentioned more medical needs, 11 per cent more social needs and 10 per cent more language and communication difficulties. While more pupils on the borderline between Moderate and Severe Learning Difficulty (SLD) are now being placed in MLD schools, advances in medical care are leading to a steady increase in the number of children with profound and multiple difficulties surviving until school age and requiring provision within the SLD sector.

At the same time, the move towards care in the community has resulted in more students with severely challenging behaviour being placed in day or residential special schools. As Russell (1997) points out, to meet the needs of such pupils a collaborative approach is required 'recognising that responsibility for supporting and helping children with challenging behaviour should not be the sole responsibility of one member of staff'. For such pupils, consistency of response is crucial and this can only be achieved via joint planning and an agreed strategy implemented by all staff working with the individual student.

Since the 1960s, as Starr and Lacey (1996) note, there have been many studies and reports which have indicated the importance of professionals from different disciplines working together to meet the needs of children with disabilities and difficulties. However, effective collaboration is not easy to achieve, particularly where different disciplines are sustained by different mind sets, distinct management structures and individual working practices. Bairstow *et al.* (1993) found contrasting approaches to pupils could create tensions within a multidisciplinary team and lead to problems for support assistants who were expected to vary their style depending on the professional leading the activity.

HMI (1991), in reviewing interdisciplinary support for young children with SEN, noted:

- poorly-coordinated services,
- poorly-defined roles,
- an absence of recognised leadership and structures,
- few opportunities for joint training,
- few opportunities to share information,
- difficulties in recruiting paramedical professionals, and
- frequent changes in personnel.

Lloyd-Smith (1995) noted the extra problems created in the 1990s by the purchaser/provider split in health service provision, which further discouraged professional collaboration. Within schools, the additional bureaucracy created by the advent of the National Curriculum and the Code of Practice has provided a further drain on the time and energy of teachers and thus a disincentive to joint planning.

Nevertheless, as Starr and Lacey (1996) note, many individual professionals still manage to organise their work to provide time for meetings, joint assessments and training. For example, Taylor *et al.* (1993) describe a multiprofessional approach to the assessment of communication skills involving joint observation by speech and language therapist, class teacher and nursery nurse. Similarly, Wright (1996) in a survey of school-based speech therapists, found 35 per cent involved in joint assessment with teachers, 47 per cent involved in joint planning and 56 per cent in joint interventions.

Where collaborative working is most successful, there is evidence of support from relevant managers. For, as Emblem (personal communication) comments: 'joint planning is essential for schools which want a team approach to children's learning'. Without such support, room management procedures frequently lapse (Woods and Cullen 1983) and role definitions become blurred to the detriment of staff morale and student progress. As Lacey and Lomas (1993) stress, the ultimate aim should be a 'commitment to teach, learn and work together across disciplines and boundaries to implement unified service plans'.

Approaches to room management

Teachers in both special and ordinary schools can be faced with a complex management task when they have to organise more than one additional adult in their classroom. Most lessons with more than one adult in support are very poorly organised in both special and ordinary schools. The establishment of a well planned but flexible network of adult roles in the classroom is a particular challenge. (Audit Commission 1992)

In most special schools, the presence of two, three or even more adults in the classroom is commonplace. In addition to the teacher there may be one or more nursery nurses, plus unqualified care assistants, volunteers, parents, students or therapists. Yet as McBrien and Weightman (1980) discovered in their study of a school for pupils with severe learning difficulties, the injection of extra adults into the classroom may have little effect on the children's learning.

Around 50 per cent of the time the activities of the additional adults in their study were of little value to either the teacher or the children and in some cases were counterproductive, for example giving undue attention to children behaving inappropriately. They attempted to tackle this problem by training staff in appropriate activities and dividing up the teacher's role to give less room for ambiguity among team members. This approach, termed 'room management' raised the adults' on-task behaviour from 48 per cent to 74 per cent and the children's engagement in work-related tasks from 30 per cent to 57 per cent.

Subsequent research by Ware and Evans (1987), in a setting for children with profound and multiple disabilities, confirmed that room management was highly effective in ensuring that all pupils received a fair share of adult attention. This was particularly important for these pupils, as those not receiving direct contact with an adult showed little increase in time on-task. However, room management has proved to be an equally effective method of deploying support staff in a whole range of different special and mainstream settings.

As Thomas (1992) comments, there are two elements of the teacher's role that are difficult to fulfil at the same time. These are the need to work with individuals and the need to work with the whole class. Where there are additional adults in the classroom on a regular basis, as in the special school, these two roles can conveniently be split and allocated to different people. In the traditional room management model three distinct roles are defined (see Figure 5.3).

ROOM MANAGEMENT

- INDIVIDUAL WORKER → Individual programmes
- MOVER → Toileting, messages, clearing up and organising equipment
- ACTIVITY MANAGER → Whole-class activities and group work

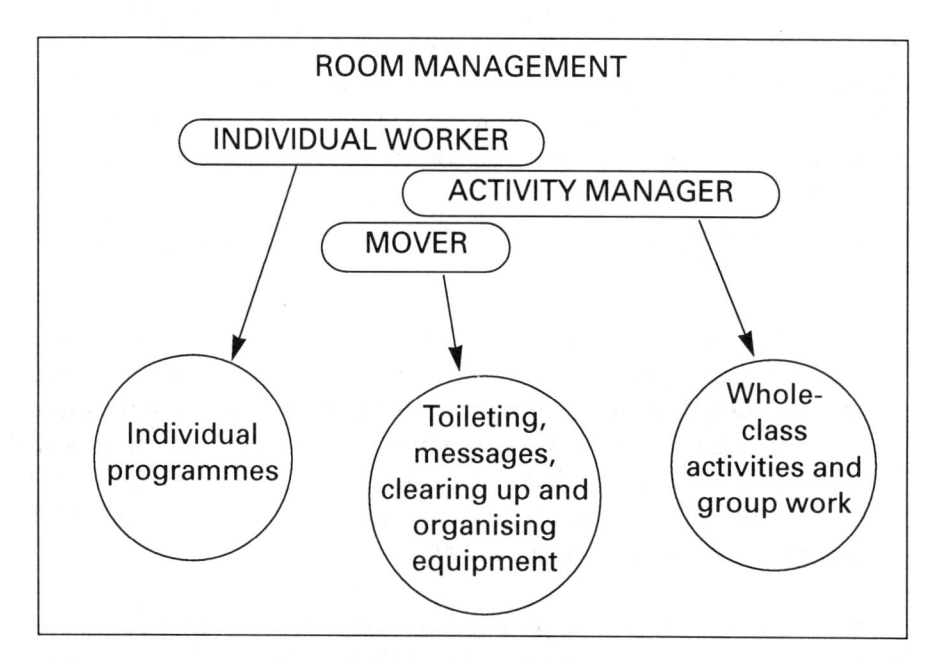

Figure 5.3

(a) The individual helper:

- concentrates on working with individual pupils, using a predetermined programme or activity, for periods of 5 to 15 minutes;
- rotates around the class, working with each child in turn on an agreed basis;

- works with children outside the main classroom or in a relatively distraction-free corner;
- takes no responsibility for other children in the class;
- ignores outside distractions, such as telephone calls, messages.

(b) The activity manager:

- concentrates on the rest of the class who would normally be in small groups working on familiar tasks;
- moves around the groups ensuring that all the pupils are actively involved in the activities set;
- avoids working intensively with any individual or group;
- remains in the classroom throughout the session;
- does not disturb the individual worker.

(c) The mover:

- fetches or organises equipment for the individual worker or activity manager;
- supervises the preparation or clearing up of activities;
- deals with interruptions, messages, etc;
- takes children to the toilet;
- supervises children moving around the school.

During a specified activity period, the individuals involved explain their role to the children and to other colleagues, to avoid embarrassment or the appearance of rudeness. In some schools, coloured badges are worn to make it clear who is taking on which role at any one time. Activity periods can last from half an hour up to half a day, although they are generally around an hour in length. In most schools, staff swap roles on a regular basis to:

- give variety to staff;
- give variety to children;
- extend staff expertise.

Where there are only two adults available, the activity manager can also take on the role of mover, although there may be problems if he or she is called out of the classroom. In such situations, it may be better to deal with messages or take pupils to the toilet before the room management period starts, or after it has ended. Where there are more than three adults, an additional individual worker or activity manager can be provided, increasing the opportunities for structured work. In setting up a room management programme, the following sequence of activities is recommended:

1. Set up a meeting with all the adults involved.
2. Decide when room management will be used and the length of the sessions.

Effective In-class Support

3. Compile a list of all the tasks that might need carrying out during that time.
4. Decide how the tasks should be shared between activity manager and mover.
5. Write out a job description for each role.
6. Set up a rota of children for individual programmes.
7. Decide how long each child should have with the individual worker.
8. Decide where the individual worker will operate.
9. Agree to set up a bank of work cards or programmes for each child, together with relevant teaching materials, which can be easily accessed by the individual worker.
10. Agree that these materials will not be moved by other members of staff.
11. Make badges for the roles.
12. Explain to colleagues about the programme.
13. Explain the programme to the children.
14. Set up a rota for each role.
15. Agree on activities for group work.
16. Try it out for a week and then meet to review progress.
17. Fine-tune the programme.
18. Update individual programmes and group activities weekly.
19. Meet to review progress on a regular basis.
20. Celebrate your successes!

Chapter 6

Putting Support on the Agenda

Although it is assumed that the majority of schools will have support systems in place, there will always be situations where additional specialist staff are required. In some LEAs, support staff are retained centrally and schools may have little part to play in their selection or deployment. Where the allocation of staff is carried out in close consultation with individual schools, this system can work well. However, where little attention is paid to the needs and wishes of the school, then relationships can break down, to the detriment of staff and students.

Because of the difficulties inherent in matching resources to need on an authority-wide basis and the progressive devolution of central funding, most LEAs now expect their schools to play a major part in selecting and appointing their own staff. However, evidence suggests that recruiting support staff can be a stressful business, particularly where schools still rely on LEA funding to pay their salaries. In many instances, the final statement does not arrive until after the child has started school or the new term is already underway. Without a guarantee of funding, schools are understandably reluctant to make new appointments or renew existing contracts. Even where appointments can be made, notice may need to be worked before newly-appointed staff can take up their posts.

When a statemented child leaves school or transfers elsewhere, experienced support staff may be left without any guarantee of further employment. Similarly, levels of support may be reduced, leaving staff with insufficient hours to meet their current expenditure. They may then be forced to seek work elsewhere and so be unavailable when a new statement arrives. Instead of building on existing partnerships, the school is obliged to start all over again with someone new.

In the best organised LEAs, statements are finalised or amended well before the start of the new school year, giving time for existing contracts to be renewed and new staff found. Even so, the task of finding suitable people is not an easy one, particularly when the child requires help on a part-time basis at specified times of the day. As Caswell (1992) comments:

Recruitment and selection

Finding suitable candidates who are able to work what are likely to be short, irregular units of time is not easy, so as a first step, it is worthwhile for schools to keep a 'long list' of possible candidates who are thought to be both skilled and available.

These may be existing volunteers or welfare staff, interested parents or others from the community who already have a good relationship with the school. However, while this may be the ideal, many schools will be unable to find sufficient suitable people locally and will need to advertise, shortlist, interview and select, all of which take time and money. An approach adopted in some LEAs with 'families of schools' (Cade and Caffyn 1995) is for the schools involved to make joint appointments and deploy those staff flexibly across the family. Staff requiring a full-time position can combine two or more part-time posts in neighbouring schools.

Nevertheless, there is often a shortage of people with the skills required to fill advertised posts, particularly those for support assistants in the secondary sector. Cheminais (1997) attempted to overcome this problem by running school-based induction courses for prospective support assistants. Similar authority-wide courses have been run in Bury where again there was a recognised shortage of assistants keen to work in the secondary sector.

Some LEAs, such as Bury, try to help their schools by maintaining a list of support teachers and assistants or by running an informal placement agency. Schools seeking support staff notify a LEA officer as do staff seeking new appointments or additional hours. Names are passed on and schools then interview and select as they see fit. In Waltham Forest (Nolan and Gersch 1996) this process has been taken one stage further; here the LEA recruits and selects a large pool of support assistants using the Psychological Service to interview potential candidates. Successful applicants are invited to visit a particular school which has requested an assistant. Although the final appointment is made by the school, psychologists retain an oversight of the assistants in their own patch.

As with any other appointment, schools should draw up a clear job specification and selection criteria. These might include familiarity with the school or particular types of experience. Some statements specify the appointment of staff with specific training, e.g. an RSA Diploma in SpLD, an NNEB certificate or Makaton training. However, as Caswell (1992) comments, job specifications should always include 'flexibility in work skills and a willingness to work jointly and collaboratively. An enthusiasm to learn new skills is important too, as well as an ability to pass these on to others'.

In her study of classroom assistants in primary schools, Moyles (1997) interviewed 15 head teachers about their selection criteria. Some were unable to be precise, making comments such as: 'I don't have any specific expectations – CAs [care assistants] come in all shapes and sizes'. Others talked of head-hunting suitable parents or 'locals we know and trust to do what we want'. Nevertheless, some criteria were used more commonly than others in the selection

SELECTION CRITERIA FOR CLASSROOM ASSISTANTS

Attribute	Responses	Selected comments
Is able to take initiative	15	'Our CA has now taken over the entire library of her own volition and out of sheer interest'
Works as team member	15	'Our CAs really are just like teaching staff – willing to take on anything'
Experienced with children	15	'We want the right people for the children, such as those who've been child minders'
Positive personality	14	'You've met her – she's such a lively and good natured person'
Adaptable	10	'They are steeped in children and willing to come to any planning meetings when we are discussing children's work'
Enthusiastic	6	'We must accept that these people primarily work for the kick they get from the job'
Willing to train	5	'They picked up the training we were giving to them and acted upon it very very quickly'
Sense of humour	5	'We can all have a laugh together when things don't go as planned'
Has a specialism	5	Such as secretarial, sports or craft skills
Intelligent	5	'We want someone we can treat like teachers'
Absorbs things quickly	4	'We need people with the ability to prevent problems happening and intervene appropriately'
Useful life skills	4	'We need people who can take the burden off teachers'

Figure 6.1

process. These are spelled out in Figure 6.1 and could apply equally well to support teachers.

Because of sporadic patterns of working, living near the school may be a real advantage both for the support worker and for the school staff who are then able to tailor the support more flexibly to meet individual needs. It may also enable the support assistant to develop a relationship with the child's family. For many schools, the building of a bridge between the parents and the school is particularly important. As Bone and Mason (1994) note, 'more often than not you [the LSA] are the direct link between child, parents/carers and teacher'. In some cases, this relationship starts with the involvement of the parents in the shortlisting and interviewing of prospective assistants.

Drawing up a job description

As numerous authors (e.g. Balshaw 1991) have noted, the lack of an adequate job description for support staff is probably the key factor leading to low job satisfaction and poor quality interventions. For, as Fox (1993) comments: 'It is frequently the case that SNAs [Special Needs Assistants] are thrown in at the deep end with no clear idea of what is expected of them. This leads to feelings of confusion and of being undervalued'. The same concerns are expressed by support teachers without a clearly-defined role. As one quoted by Thomas (1992) states: 'You can't just pick somebody up and throw them into a room and say "Now on you go and support"'.

If, as Moyles (1997) suggests, the majority of teachers and classroom assistants perceive the assistant's role differently, conflicts are bound to arise. Balshaw (1991) talks of assistants being 'piggy in the middle', caught between the teacher and the child. As one assistant says:

> Nobody has explained to me properly what I'm supposed to do. I've been picking it up as I go along. Sometimes, but not regularly, I'm given instructions at the start of the day. And I haven't got a proper job description, only a vague one I got with my contract, it's not much practical use. Nobody refers to it anyway, and it's been like this for nearly four terms now.

Much the same situation can arise in the case of support teachers (Lovey 1995), who may be prevented from doing their job as they see it or be asked to undertake inappropriate tasks. The only sensible way round this is for support staff to be given a job description that specifies their duties and responsibilities in such a way that is clear to all concerned. A job description should have two main elements as defined by Fox (1993):

1. Ground rules for working with the teacher.
2. An individual plan for the child or children being supported.

Where there is likely to be input or advice from more than one key professional, it is vital that the support worker knows whose directions to follow. In such cases, the SENCO has a responsibility to ensure that advice from the class teacher, subject teachers, advisory staff, therapists and psychologist is coordinated in such a way as to avoid conflict. Even then, it is essential that support workers, particularly where they have few qualifications and limited training, know who they should refer to on a day-to-day basis and this line management responsibility should be spelled out in the job description.

In drawing up a job description for an existing member of staff, the sequence of actions described in Figure 6.2 is recommended. The resulting job description (see 'Model', Figure 6.3, and 6.4 a proforma) should include:

- those duties and responsibilities common to all members of the school community,
- those duties which are particular to the role of LSA, Support Teacher, Bilingual Language Assistant, etc., and
- those duties which relate to the individual's specific job.

Where a new post is being created or a new appointment made, an outline job description should already be available in draft form, to ensure that candidates are quite clear about what is involved. Once

---

DRAWING UP A NEW JOB DESCRIPTION

Support assistants or support teachers, working individually or as a group, list all their current duties

↓

Together with their SENCO, they discuss the lists and agree the core responsibilities

↓

The SENCO draws up a general job description, which is then shared with the school's senior management team and with teaching staff, at a full staff meeting

↓

A final job description is drawn up for each individual assistant or support teacher

↓

Job descriptions are renegotiated at least annually, with feedback from both the staff concerned and the teachers they support

---

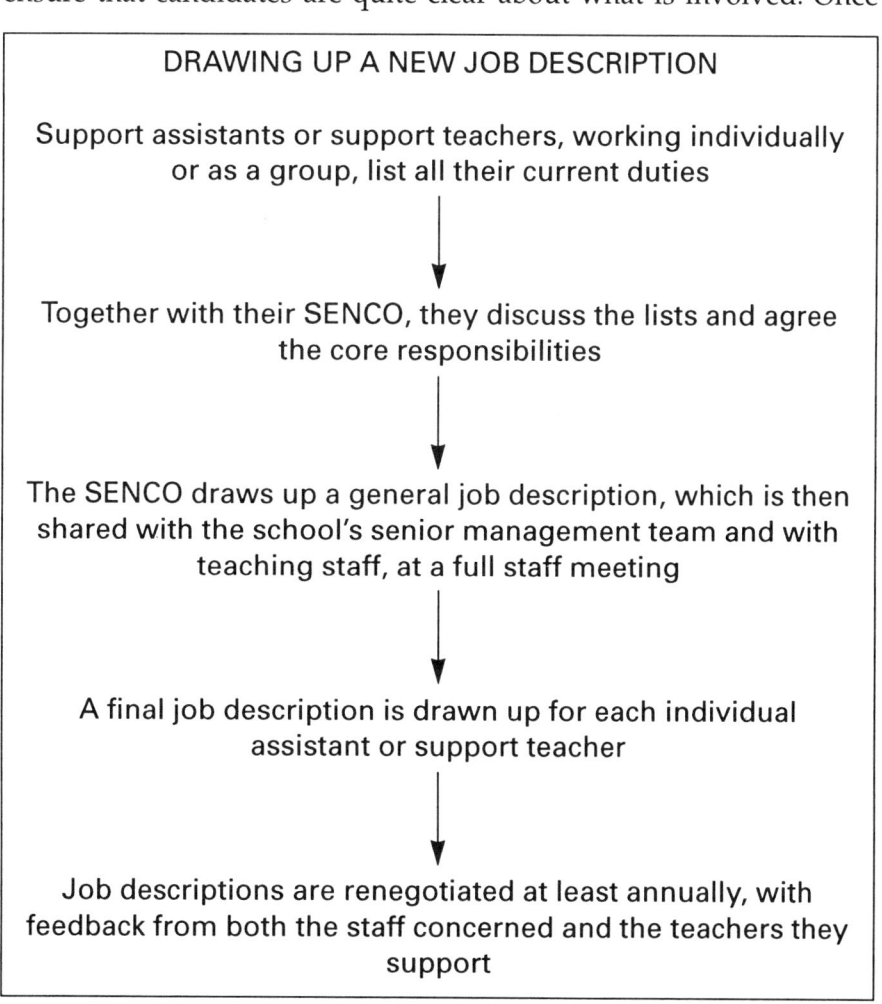

Figure 6.2

Effective In-class Support

MODEL JOB DESCRIPTION
(Courtesy of Bury MBC)

Post title: Special Support Assistant

Department: Education   Post grade: Nursery staff in educational establishments

Location: Holly Primary School   Post hours: 20 hours (9.30–11.30 + 1.30–3.30)

Purpose and objectives of post: To support Marie Saunders, help boost her learning skills and help her gain in independence

Accountable to: Governing body and head teacher

Immediately responsible to: Mr Walker (Class teacher)

Special conditions of service:
(a) Appointment may be terminated by either party giving one week's notice in writing
(b) Holidays must be taken during periods of school closure
(c) School must be notified immediately in case of sickness or unavoidable absence
(d) Opportunities for in-service training will be provided

Relationships: Mrs Gordon (SENCO)
All other staff and pupils of the school
Mr and Mrs Saunders (Marie's parents)
Ms Francis (Speech Therapist)
Miss Bedford (Learning Support Service)
Mr Thomas (Educational Psychologist)

Control of resources:
(a) Learning materials for Marie and other pupils in her group
(b) Marie's speech therapy programme
(c) Books and equipment borrowed from Learning Support Service

Figure 6.3 (*continued on next page*)

DUTIES and RESPONSIBILITIES

Support for pupils:
(a) To implement a language development programme daily, as detemined by Speech and Language Therapist
(b) To provide help with basic skills in a small group
(c) To offer help, as appropriate, to any pupil experiencing difficulties
(d) To ensure that Marie works independently for periods of up to 10 minutes throughout the day
(e) To offer Marie regular praise and encouragement

Support for the teacher:
(a) To assist in the production of teaching and learning materials for Marie and other pupils with SEN
(b) To assist in the development and implementation of appropriate systems for recording progress of pupils with SEN
(c) To assist in the management of the whole class
(d) To provide regular feedback to Mr Walker (Class teacher)

Support for the school:
(a) To foster home school liaison for pupils with SEN
(b) To contribute to Annual Review procedure
(c) To contribute to the evaluation of the school's SEN policy and practice by discussions with relevant staff
(d) To attend appropriate in-service training provided by school or LEA
(e) To be aware of and follow school policies and procedures

Other duties: To carry out any other relevant tasks as directed by the head teacher, SENCO or class teacher

Agreed by postholder: Hilary Martin

Agreed by supervisor: Mark Walker   Date: 10.9.98.

Figure 6.3 (*continuation*)

Effective In-class Support

JOB DESCRIPTION

Post title:

Department: Post grade:

Location: Post hours:

Purpose and objectives of post:

Accountable to:

Immediately responsible to:

Special conditions of service:

Relationships:

Control of resources:

Figure 6.4 (*continued on next page*)

DUTIES and RESPONSIBILITIES

Support for pupils:

Support for the teacher:

Support for the school:

Other duties:

Agreed by postholder:

Agreed by supervisor: Date:

Figure 6.4 (*continuation*)

appointed, they should be given the opportunity to comment upon the job description and where appropriate, suggest modifications. Good job descriptions are:

- individual,
- up to date,
- unambiguous,
- accessible.

They should also be reviewed on a regular basis to ensure that they:

- meet the child's changing needs,
- continue to meet the needs of the class or subject teacher,
- constitute an effective use of resources,
- make appropriate demands on the postholder.

Existing job descriptions can be reviewed individually or in a group setting, with both the postholder and the teachers they support involved.

> Last week we had a meeting involving the assistants and the teachers who work with them... It was ever so useful, and everybody will now have an individual meeting to discuss with the teacher they most work with, to review their job descriptions, and how the daily routine fits into them, and write something down, so we can review it together at the end of term. I've been feeling so positive since then, it's great to work and plan with the teachers about what we do. I'm a lot happier now. (Support assistant quoted in Balshaw 1991)

Wherever possible, the parents of pupils with statements and the individual pupils themselves should also be consulted, particularly if changes in the delivery of the support package are envisaged. Such discussions can help to reduce parental concerns or even formal complaints when parents discover, for example, that their child's support assistant will no longer be working with them individually but in a group, in an effort to increase their independence. Evaluation of job descriptions can also form an effective part of the appraisal process for support staff, as well as leading to improvements in the policy and practice of the school as a whole.

Building effective teams

Good teamwork is notoriously difficult to achieve. In industry, an enormous research effort on the workings of teams attests to the truth of this fact. In education, also, the difficulty in making teams effective is conspicuous. (Thomas 1992)

As Bartholomew and Bruce (1993) point out: 'when adults come together and use their energy in an orchestrated way on behalf of the child, then quality and excellent progress are seen'. In an effective team (Nias *et al.* 1989):

- Each member's function contributes to the team task.
- Each member feels responsible to the team and is valued by it.
- Each member responds flexibly to emergent team needs as s/he perceives them.
- Leading the team carries obligations as well as powers.

All organisations have both formal and informal communication systems and this is just as true for the small village school as it is for the large comprehensive. Formal systems may comprise a staff handbook, a daily briefing from the head teacher, or a series of *ad hoc* notices on a board. Informal systems may consist of casual groupings in the staffroom over coffee or in the pub after school. With such a complex flow of information around the school, it is all too easy for support staff, many of whom are part-time, to get left in what Balshaw (1991) describes as 'no man's land'.

Ensuring that all staff are on the circulation list for written communications is relatively straightforward. Similarly, including attendance at whole-staff or departmental meetings within the contracted time of the support teacher or assistant can be highly cost-effective. To raise their profile in the school, photographs of assistants should always be part of the display in the entrance hall and their names entered on staff lists. Supply staff also need to be made aware when an assistant or support teacher will be in their lesson and the way in which they normally work.

Some schools produce guidelines for teaching staff on the use of support personnel, although as Mortimore *et al.* (1994) note, this is surprisingly rare. In one comprehensive school quoted by them, the support assistants are given a leaflet which provides guidance on:

- school protocol,
- appropriate ways of interacting with pupils, teachers and parents,
- advice on teamwork,
- staff development opportunities.

At the same time, teaching staff are issued with a companion leaflet setting out management responsibilities for staff working with them. To help schools develop such guidance, some LEAs issue information booklets to schools at the same time as a new statement is finalised. In Bury, schools receive a leaflet entitled *The Induction of Special Support Assistants* (Bury 1996) which includes suggested procedures to be followed after appointment (see Figure 6.5).

In the absence of a whole-school approach to support, individual teachers will need to develop their own response. Challen and Majors (1997) provide helpful checklists for teachers working with special support assistants, as well as for the support assistants themselves. These include questions such as:

- Have you arranged to meet with your SSA before the starting date?
- Have you talked through the organisation of your class, day, week?
- Can you set aside a regular time to meet with your SSA to discuss planning, progress and problems?

Effective In-class Support

GUIDELINES FOLLOWING APPOINTMENT
(Courtesy of Bury MBC)

1. SSAs should be given a clear job description

2. SSAs should be introduced to staff who should be made aware of their role within the school

3. SSAs should be made aware of the procedures within the school, e.g. behaviour, rules, injuries, parental contact

4. SSAs should be given access to the statement and any relevant information on the child's specific condition

5. SSAs should be given time to meet with class teachers and plan the timetable, which should include time for liaison and preparation

6. SSAs should know the ground rules for working with a class teacher – these may vary from school to school

7. SSAs should be given information about the school year/calendar

8. SSAs should be given any help necessary, e.g. completing salary claims, transport information

---

Figure 6.5

Exactly the same questions could be addressed in relation to partnership with a departmental colleague, an SEN support teacher or a member of the English Language Teaching Service. As team members, the two adults must:

- support each other,
- give the same message to the pupils,
- deal with misbehaviour in the same way.

To do this, it is essential that the class teacher and the support worker communicate. However, in many schools joint planning is not given the priority it deserves and staff find it extremely difficult to meet on a regular basis. Lee and Henkhuzens (1996) found joint planning limited by:

- non-teaching periods for subject and support staff occurring at different times;
- support assistants being unable to stay after school;
- teachers reluctant to put too much responsibility on support staff;
- teachers without the time to plan their lessons sufficiently in advance.

Yet, as Mortimore *et al.* (1994) comment: 'For staff providing in-class support to have to rely on ad hoc day-to-day instructions is wasteful. For them to be denied feedback on their work can be educationally inefficient and personally demoralising'. Where senior managers are prepared to build planning time into the school programme, the following schedule of meetings is recommended.

At the beginning of the year, the teacher and support worker need to agree:

- introductions: how will the job of the support teacher or assistant be explained to pupils?
- roles and responsibilities: who will do what?
- discipline: what methods to use?
- teaching methods: e.g. hearing children read.
- the needs of individual pupils in the teaching group.

When new work is being introduced, they need to:

- look at the books and materials to be used, so that the support worker knows what is expected;
- agree what particular help any individual or group of pupils should have.

In one support team, described by Doyle (1997), there was a 30-minute meeting before school once a fortnight. A formal agenda was used covering four categories of item:

1. training needs for the LSA, class teacher or SENCO,
2. issues affecting the whole class,
3. forthcoming lessons and teaching topics,
4. individual student needs.

Even where regular meetings are held, support staff need to give feedback to subject teachers on an ongoing basis. However, many people feel uncomfortable in raising their concerns. While this problem is particularly acute for unqualified classroom assistants, it can apply equally to experienced teachers working in a support role. As one teacher quoted by Thomas (1992) states:

> I think you have to be very careful, you can't go in and try and change the world if you have to fit into their model. If you think there should be changes or you have suggestions, do it over a period of time or you would get people's backs up.

Induction and basic training

Many support assistants come into post with little experience of schools or of special needs. While they may have a wealth of experience with their own or other people's children, they will need careful induction before they start work (Clayton *et al.* 1989). Equally, support teachers who are new to the school, or who have been out of teaching for some time, may also benefit from a basic induction package, although this may be rather different to that offered to classroom assistants. Pothecary and McCarthy (1996) recommend a ten-day induction programme for new support staff.

Day 1:

- Introduce support assistant to key members of staff.
- Provide essential documentation, e.g. timings of school day, staff list, fire drill, school behaviour policy, etc.
- Take SSA on tour of school and allow time for questions.
- Introduce SSA to child or children with whom he or she will be working.
- Allow SSA to observe class in which he or she will be working.

Day 2:

- Give handbook, to be read briefly in school and taken home for further study.
- Provide SSA with details of pupils with whom they will be working.
- Discuss the support role with regard to the child.
- Make arrangements for the SSA to meet the parents.
- Allow the SSA to spend the rest of the day in a general support role.

Day 3:

- Explain the whole-school support role, including health and safety regulations.
- Give the SSA a personal timetable.
- In the primary school, provide time for the class teacher to discuss roles and responsibilities with the SSA.
- In the secondary school give the SSA time with each subject teacher they are to work with (this may take several days).
- Give the SSA time to read any materials given out.

Day 4:

- Begin the timetable.
- Check at break or lunchtime that everything is all right.

Days 5–9

- Continue timetable.
- Be available when required, to deal with any queries.

Day 10:

- Arrange a meeting between the SSA and the SENCO to review the schedule of work given.
- Provide job description to discuss and then sign.
- Decide on future needs and schedule to address them.
- Give guidance on line management responsibilities, grievance procedures, etc.
- Schedule a meeting for a detailed look at the child's IEP.

In schools where there is more than one support assistant, new staff can shadow a more experienced colleague for a day or two before starting their own timetable. Alternatively, newly-appointed staff can be allocated a mentor to whom they can take their concerns and worries. Bedfordshire (OPTIS 1992) have produced a useful manual for teachers taking on this role.

In some schools (Macauley 1998), mentoring is delegated to a senior support assistant who is responsible for the welfare of the support team and is paid at a slightly higher rate, in recognition of this responsibility. While common among lunchtime supervisors, such a hierarchy is rare in school support teams, but may represent an appropriate way of providing a career structure for experienced assistants who have no desire to undertake further formal training or enter the teaching profession.

In addition to providing an induction programme within school, to ease the new entrant into the job, some schools ensure that newly-appointed staff receive a basic INSET package, covering the key skills they will need. In some cases this training is provided by the LEA, in others it is delivered by the school itself. Thus in Leeds (Lorenz 1992) a five-module programme was offered on one half day per week, covering:

- special needs and the law
- the role of the support assistant
- managing difficult behaviour
- supporting children's learning
- raising self-esteem and working in a team.

In Waltham Forest (Nolan and Gersch 1996) induction training lasted two days and included opportunities for newly-appointed staff to consider equal opportunities issues, discuss case studies and look at record-keeping, as well as covering principles of support and behaviour management. In Bury, the induction programme for prospective secondary assistants lasted two weeks and included four days of job shadowing in a school. Cheminais's school-based taster programme, on the other hand (Cheminais 1997), was spread over six evenings, with one module per week lasting 1½ hours.

These programmes and many others like them, have been based to a large extent on the pioneering work of Terry Clayton in Wiltshire (Clayton 1990). As early as 1988, he and his colleagues realised the importance of training for the growing body of unqualified staff in mainstream schools and established their SAINTS, programme (Clayton *et al.* 1989) which has served as a model for most of the courses that followed it. Where induction training has not been available, staff have been encouraged to read training packages such as the *Handbook for Special Needs Assistants* (Fox 1993), *Special Support Assistants: A Manual for Schools* (Pothecary and McCarthy 1997) or *The Support Assistant's Survival Guide* (Lorenz 1998b).

All these materials provide useful background for newly-appointed personnel. However, they are insufficient on their own to replace a properly organised course which will allow support staff to:

- meet with others taking on a similar role;
- explore their prejudices and preconceptions in a safe environment;
- ask questions about their future role and air any concerns;
- receive input tailored to their particular needs;
- find out about their particular LEA and the services available;
- meet members of the LEA support services;
- identify further training and support needs;
- establish mutually supportive alliances with colleagues.

Chapter 7

Support Systems for Support Staff

The importance of health and safety, both for ancillary staff and for the children they work with, must never be forgotten in developing any programme of support. Students with medical problems or physical disabilities can be vulnerable, not only in the playground and moving around the school building, but also in a busy classroom. A balance between safety and independence can be difficult to achieve and will require considerable thought and planning from the whole-school team. The involvement of the parents and the pupil is also vital if the needs of all concerned are to be addressed.

Schools have a legal duty to take all reasonable steps to safeguard the wellbeing of staff and pupils (see Gold and Szemerenyi 1998). Only in the case of negligence will a parent be able to take action against the school. As long as a support teacher or assistant is carrying out duties connected with the job, then it is their employer who is liable for any harm, loss or injury caused by their actions. Nevertheless, certain safeguards should always be in place.

Unqualified support staff should never be left in sole charge of an individual pupil or group of children. Even where an activity takes place outside the classroom, the assistant should always know which teacher is ultimately in charge and how they can be contacted in an emergency. Lessons should be conducted in a safe manner, and support staff who are asked to work with unfamiliar equipment, or to supervise physical activities, must insist on being properly trained and supervised.

Where support staff are expected to lift or handle pupils, appropriate training should always be provided. The Manual Handling Operations Regulations (HSE 1992) made under the Safety at Work Act 1974 came into force in January 1993. These suggest that employees should, where possible, avoid hazardous manual handling operations. Where these cannot be avoided, a thorough risk assessment should be carried out (see Figure 7.1) and action taken to minimise risk of injury (see Figure 7.2).

Everyone should be familiar with fire procedures and involved in

Health and safety issues

Effective In-class Support

RISK ASSESSMENT CHECKLIST
(Courtesy of the Disabled Living Centre, Manchester)

A. THE PUPIL

Name:
Approximate weight: Approximate height:
Age: Class:

1. Is the pupil difficult to handle due to:
   (a) restrictive clothing?   Y   N
   (b) impaired mental state?   Y   N
   (c) physical incapacities?   Y   N
   (d) their size, weight or shape?   Y   N
   (e) unpredictable physical movement?   Y   N
   (f) unpredictable behaviour?   Y   N

2. Is the pupil unable or unwilling to assist with the   Y   N
   manoeuvre?

3. Is this due to pain, fatigue, weakness, stiffness, anxiety,
   inability to understand you?(circle where appropriate)

Risk identified:

B. THE ENVIRONMENT

1. Does lack of space inhibit/prevent good working posture
   due to:
   (a) size or height of desk, work area?   Y   N
   (b) obstructive furniture?   Y   N
   (c) room size?   Y   N
   (d) other children?   Y   N

2. Are there irregular, slippery or cluttered floors?   Y   N

3. Do poor lighting conditions affect safety?   Y   N

4. Does handler's clothing impede the use of safe   Y   N
   techniques?

5. Is handling equipment inaccessible?   Y   N

Risk identified:

Figure 7.1 (*continued on next page*)

Support Systems for Support Staff

C. TASK		
1. Is it absolutely necessary to perform a manual handling manoevre?	Y	N
2. Does the task involve high stress movement?	Y	N
3. Are these postures sustained for lengthy periods?	Y	N
4. Does the task involve:		
(a) excessive lifting or lowering distances?	Y	N
(b) excessive carrying distances?	Y	N
(c) excessive pushing or pulling of the person (including a hoist)?	Y	N
5. Is the child held away from the handler's body?	Y	N
6. Is there a risk that the child will move suddenly?	Y	N
7. Does the task involve more than one manoeuvre or lift in each take over episode of care?	Y	N
8. Does the task involve two or more handlers?	Y	N
9. Does the task involve the use of mechanical handling equipment or mechanical aids?	Y	N

Risk identified:

D. INDIVIDUAL CAPACITY

1. Does the task put at risk handlers who are pregnant or who have ill health?	Y	N
2. Does the task put at risk those who have musculo-skeletal disorders?	Y	N
3. Does the task require training or knowledge over and above that covered in the basic training?	Y	N
4. Does the age of the staff put them at risk?	Y	N
5. How experienced is the carer?	Y	N

Risk identified:

Figure 7.1 (*continuation*)

PRINCIPLES OF SAFE MOVING AND HANDLING

1. Ask yourself, 'Why am I doing this? Do I need this task? Can I move this child another way?'

2. Never manually lift unless you have to.

3. Assess the child to be moved and know about their special needs. Discuss with another SSA, if necessary, the most suitable transfer.

4. Explain your intentions to the child. They will tell you if they are uncomfortable.

5. Consider the child's weight. You may need help.

6. Consider the environment. Note the hazards. Prepare first.

7. Know your own capabilities and those of your colleagues.

8. Use appropriate aids.

9. Decide on a leader if two or more of you are moving a load.

10. Commands must be understood by all.

11. You must move together on the set command.

12. Foot positions are important:
    You must have a stable base
    You must have a comfortable hand-hold for you and the child
    Hold the child as close as possible
    Keep your natural spinal curves and do not twist your trunk
    Have your knees relaxed and flexed
    Use strong leg muscles to do the work, not weak back muscles
    Keep your head up and lead with your head
    Move in stages if necessary
    Take care in lowering

Figure 7.2

fire drills. Where support staff work on a part-time basis, care should be taken to hold fire practices at times when they are at work.

Support staff should be made aware of the school's record-keeping procedures following an injury or accident or where detailed and up-to-date records of medical procedures may be required. They should also be fully briefed about any warning signs which might indicate a deterioration or change in the physical condition of any child they might be supporting.

Support staff should not be expected to administer medication unless written guidelines have been produced by the school or the LEA. While some people are happy to give medication, it must remain a voluntary activity, unless the expectation was made clear to prospective candidates before they were appointed. UNISON recommends that:

- a proforma is produced by the school and signed by parents, giving details of the medication and how it should be administered;
- the head teacher has overall responsibility for administering drugs;
- two members of staff are present when drugs are being administered;
- a written record of drugs administered is kept;
- only prescribed drugs, which are clearly labelled, are given.

First aid facilities should always be available, together with the names of qualified staff. In many schools, this role is taken by a nursery nurse or support assistant. If so, any additional duties should be included in their job description. On some occasions, it may be necessary for a support assistant to accompany a child off the premises. To ensure that insurance cover is not invalidated, it is important that such action is only taken at the direct request of a teacher. Wherever possible, the parents should be informed and their permission obtained. If support assistants carry children in their own cars, appropriate insurance is essential.

All support staff should be aware of the school's child protection policy and be vigilant to signs of physical or sexual abuse. Anecdotal evidence suggests that it is those adults in closest contact with the child who are most likely to notice or be told when they are being abused. It is vital that all staff are clear what information they can keep confidential and what needs to be passed on to someone in authority. Support staff should also receive training in the recognition of drug taking or solvent abuse by pupils and be clear when information should be recorded.

In some circumstances, particularly in the special school sector, support staff may be asked or may feel it necessary to restrain a pupil or use force to move them from one place to another. Hewitt and Arnett (1996) suggest that there are in fact few situations where the use of force is justified. The guidance accompanying the Children Act 1989 (DoH 1992) makes it clear that physical control should be avoided whenever possible. While there is little guidance for schools on what methods are permissible, they could usefully consult the document *Permissible Forms of Control in Children's Residential Care* (DoH 1993).

Physical restraint should only be used when staff have good grounds for believing that immediate action is necessary to prevent children from significantly injuring themselves or others or causing serious damage to property. Force should never be used purely to achieve compliance with staff instructions, as such use is liable to leave the adult at risk of prosecution for assault. A detailed care plan should always be drawn up between the school and the child's parents or carers. In addition, training should be given to staff working with pupils displaying challenging behaviour (e.g. Harris and Hewett 1996), which offers positive alternatives to the traditional 'confront and dominate' approach.

Supervision and appraisal

While there is little that most schools can do about the poor salaries or limited career opportunities of many ancillary staff, they *can* provide high quality support. To function effectively, staff need to know that help and advice are available when required, either from a class or subject teacher, from the SENCO or from a visiting professional (Clayton 1993). As Lally (1991) comments:

> Schools need to create an environment where individuals can feel a sense of personal achievement. In order to remain motivated, individuals need to feel that their achievements are recognised and that they are making a valuable contribution to the team.

Clear line management is essential, so that support staff are not confused and disempowered by contradictory messages from different sources (Fletcher-Campbell 1992). Where guidance on teaching strategies or approaches is being provided by professionals outside the school, it is important to ensure that this advice is mediated via the head or SENCO. Without such intervention, the support teacher or assistant may face conflicts between the outside advice and the practices or preferences of the class teacher with whom they are being expected to work. Even then, some differences of opinion may occur between teacher and support worker. One typical scenario is described by Fletcher-Campbell (1992):

> In another school there was a difference of opinion between the teachers and the assistants about what was expected of pupils with disabilities in mobility and independence. The classroom assistants tended to be strict with the pupils and to insist that they should move about the school with little help. The teaching staff argued, however, that the physical effort for pupils with severe mobility difficulties was such that, when they arrived at their next lesson,

they were not in a state conducive to learning. This particular situation could probably have been argued either way; what was undesirable was that the problem had not been faced and negotiated with an agreed policy.

As junior members of the team, support teachers or assistants may feel powerless to comment when they feel the teacher is being less than sympathetic to the child in their charge, or is making inappropriate demands. At such times, it is important that the support assistant has somewhere to turn. A SENCO, head teacher or advisory teacher who meets regularly with support workers, individually or as a group can:

- provide a safe forum in which concerns can be aired;
- offer individual counselling or advice;
- intervene to resolve conflicts;
- act as an advocate for the support worker;
- take ongoing issues to the school's senior management team.

Support teachers and assistants themselves can provide mutual support, when they meet regularly and share concerns. Common issues can be conveyed to the SENCO or head teacher far more effectively by a united front, than by any one individual. Such support groups can be facilitated within a large school, on an area basis (Lorenz 1992), or across a small LEA. In Leeds, for example, a joint approach to the LEA resulted in an official change of title from 'Non-Teaching Assistant' to 'Special Needs Assistant'. In some areas, support staff without a teaching qualification have, individually or as a group joined UNISON. Others have formed their own professional body now named CLASS.

Schools or LEAs concerned about improving the effective use of support staff are now beginning to look at the development of appraisal programmes. With the advent of the 1986 Education Act (DES 1986), appraisal became an accepted mechanism for the professional development of teachers. While few LEAs adopted similar procedures for ancillary staff, the benefits, both for staff and the organisations they work in, are clearly just the same. Bell (1988) in her study of one Northern LEA found that three quarters of her sample would have welcomed an informal appraisal of their efforts.

Pardoe and Attfield (1989), in their review of appraisal in two Salford special schools, stressed the importance of including support assistants in the process, particularly where schools have worked hard to break down the barriers between teachers and assistants. Nevertheless, HMI (DES 1992), in their survey of non-teaching staff in schools, found the effectiveness of many to be limited by 'a lack of formal or informal appraisal of performance'.

The aims of any staff appraisal system (Watmough 1986), should be to:

- provide staff with an opportunity to review their own performance and to discuss this with their immediate superior;

- improve communication between the individual and the manager;
- allow managers to identify particular strengths and interests of individuals which can be put to good effect in future planning;
- provide an opportunity for individuals to receive feedback on their performance;
- stimulate an individual to better performance;
- provide an opportunity to counsel staff on problems related to work;
- identify training and other development needs of staff;
- provide an opportunity for the individual to discuss future developments and career prospects;
- provide information required for a wider review of service provision.

An effective appraisal system contains five elements (Haykin and Pierce 1989). These are outlined in Figure 7.3. The model recommended is a triadic one, involving another assistant or teacher to mediate between the main appraiser and the person being appraised. As Pardoe and Attfield (1989) point out, this approach 'stresses the support needed for staff development and lessens the hierarchical emphasis of appraisal as something which happens to subordinates'. The triadic model allows the class or subject teacher to be involved in the appraisal process, as well as the SENCO or a member of the senior management team, fostering the development of a team approach.

THE APPRAISAL PROCESS

Preliminary Discussion
setting parameters for the appraisal

↓

Self Appraisal
using an agreed checklist

Classroom Observation
at an agreed time

↓

Appraisal Interview
giving time for both appraiser and appraisee to raise issues

↓

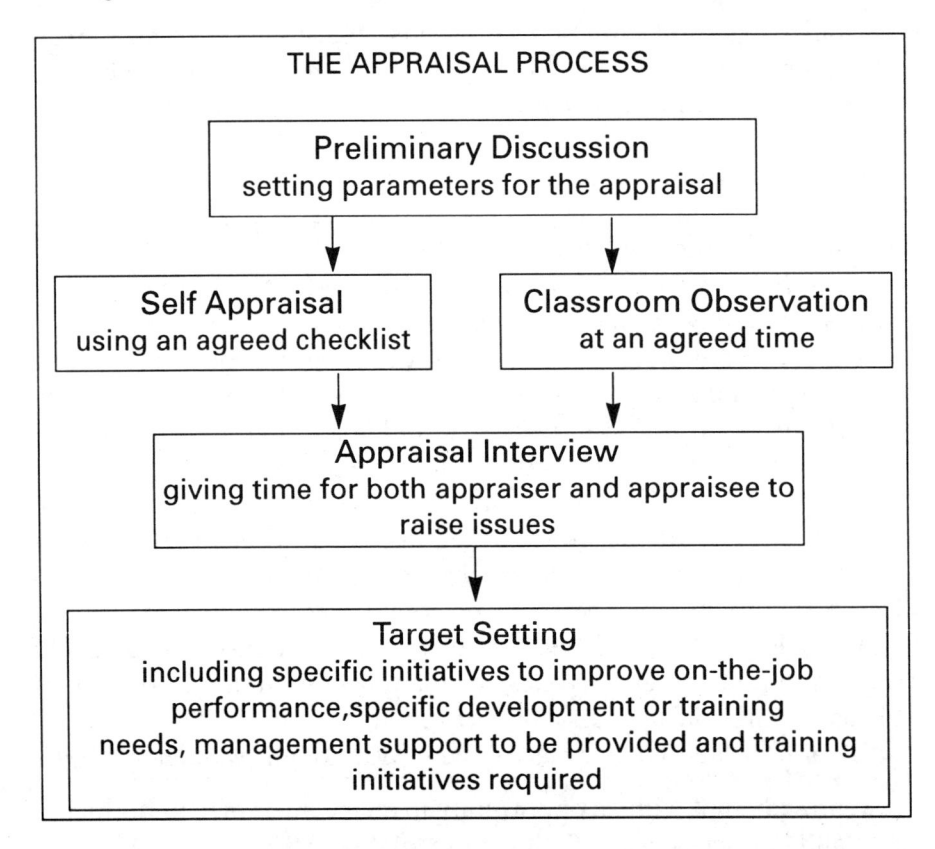

Target Setting
including specific initiatives to improve on-the-job performance, specific development or training needs, management support to be provided and training initiatives required

Figure 7.3

Data from classroom observation derived from more than one source is likely to be more acceptable to the person being observed, while the encouragement of a colleague may be essential if support workers are to feel confident in completing a self-evaluation, the framework for which can be found in Figure 7.4.

SELF-APPRAISAL CHECKLIST

1. What aspects of your job interest you most?

2. What particular aspects interest you least?

3. How do you feel about the main tasks you are responsible for?

4. Which parts of your job do you feel you could perform more effectively and how?

5. What, if any, were the reasons preventing you from being more effective in these areas?

6. What tasks do you feel you have performed particularly well and why?

7. What extra help or guidance do you feel you need to do your present job more effectively?

8. How would you like your work to change in the coming year?

9. What long-term career plans do you have?

10. What help do you need to realise them?

Figure 7.4

Continuing professional development

The importance of ongoing training for all staff involved in creating educational opportunities for children with SEN is an issue that has been highlighted by the Teacher Training Agency. Not only are competencies for SENCOs being reviewed, but general SEN awareness is to be included both in Initial Teacher Training and in the new professional qualification for head teachers. The provision of relevant training for support teachers is also a key issue in many LEAs. While most teachers working directly with SEN pupils are likely to have access to specific skill-based training (see Inglese 1996), relatively few receive training in the advisory and collaborative aspects of their role. However, as Hart (1991) notes, 'The success of their contribution to the work of teachers and schools is dependent . . . upon the expertise which they are able to bring to the collaborative process'.

While the training for support assistants has been afforded a higher profile with the publication of the recent Green Paper (DfEE 1997a), the issues here are far from being resolved. As the Government notes, fewer than half of all LEAs provide appropriate training for their support staff, despite high quality programmes having been available in some areas for many years. In Wiltshire, for example, Clayton (1990) carried out an authority-wide survey, which revealed that at least two thirds of the assistants considered that they were in need of further training. The result was the excellent SAINTS package (Clayton *et al.* 1989).

At much the same time, Oxfordshire developed a comprehensive set of training materials for its support assistants (OPTIS 1988), which is still widely used today. Similar initiatives were established in Solihull (Carpenter and Shoesmith 1991), in Calderdale (ALSS 1991), in Cambridgeshire (Balshaw 1991) and in Leeds (Lorenz 1992). In the early days, LSA training tended to focus on basic teaching approaches and on behaviour management. Largely centre-based, courses combined skill teaching with the welcome opportunity for ancillary staff, often isolated in their own schools, to meet and share experiences.

From these sessions emerged the need to look at the role of the assistant more generally and to address essential management issues. A key element of the Leeds and Cambridgeshire courses was the involvement of teaching staff in LSA training. The concept of joint training for support assistants and class teachers was taken one stage further in Northumberland, where the SENAT materials (Caswell and Pinner 1996) were developed. These comprise a series of units designed for pairs of staff to work through together, within their own school. As they note:

> The teacher/SENA pairing is viewed by the authors as being the most potent and powerful study combination. This facility for joint training not only allows an opportunity for the skills of the SENA and teacher to be enhanced through cooperative and supportive learning, but it also affords staff an opportunity to develop a consistent and coordinated approach.

While this package is one of the most comprehensive produced to date, there are drawbacks to staff working on their own, without either tutorial support or the opportunity to share with colleagues in other schools. However, there is no reason why staff using these materials could not be encouraged to join together on a termly or half-termly basis, with the aid of a facilitator, to air concerns and provide mutual support.

Where the SENAT materials are designed for joint work, a number of other schemes incorporate specific training activities for class teachers or SENCOs working with or managing ancillary staff. The Bedfordshire materials (OPTIS 1992), for example, include a guide for mentors. In much the same vein, the training manual by Pothecary and McCarthy 1996 has two separate sections, one for school managers and the other for support assistants. The present author has also adopted a similar approach, producing two companion volumes *Supporting Support Assistants* (Lorenz 1996) for SENCOs and senior managers and *The Support Assistant's Survival Guide* (Lorenz 1998b) for the assistants themselves.

With a growing number of different courses on offer, the issue of quality control is of increasing importance, and with it the need to establish a pattern of accredited training that will have national currency. Although no national standards are yet in place, many colleges of Further Education now offer the City and Guilds Certificate in Learning Support. Unfortunately, while the framework and the expected competencies are clearly spelled out, the quality of input and supervision offered varies widely from one institution to another.

In other areas, courses accredited by the Open College Network are available, while some establishments, such as Manchester Metropolitan University, accredit LEA-run courses, which can be used as an entry qualification for further training. Some colleges offer programmes leading to NVQ Level 3, while still others run higher level courses such as the Government-initiated STA programme (Moyles 1997). In the face of the plethora of different training routes available (see Figure 7.5) there is, clearly, an urgent need for rationalisation and with it a guarantee of both induction and ongoing training of a high standard for all support staff. Once accredited courses are universal, other LEAs might adopt the approach employed in Bury and offer an extra salary increment to all those who have successfully completed a recognised programme of training.

However, addressing the training needs of support staff and their managers is not enough, if schools are to adopt a coordinated approach. Balshaw (1991) makes this point in promoting 'collaborative enquiry' across an entire school. If class and subject teachers do not know how to use support to best effect, then there is little point in training ancillary staff. As one assistant said, on a recent training course run by the author: 'It's all very well training us, but what about training them?'

```
                TRAINING ROUTES FOR SUPPORT ASSISTANTS

                          Specialist
                          Teaching
                          Assistant
             Open          course         NVQ
            College                       Level 3
            course
                          SUPPORT
                          ASSISTANT
           Certificate
           in Learning                    LEA-run
           Support       University-      programme
                         accredited
                         certificate
```

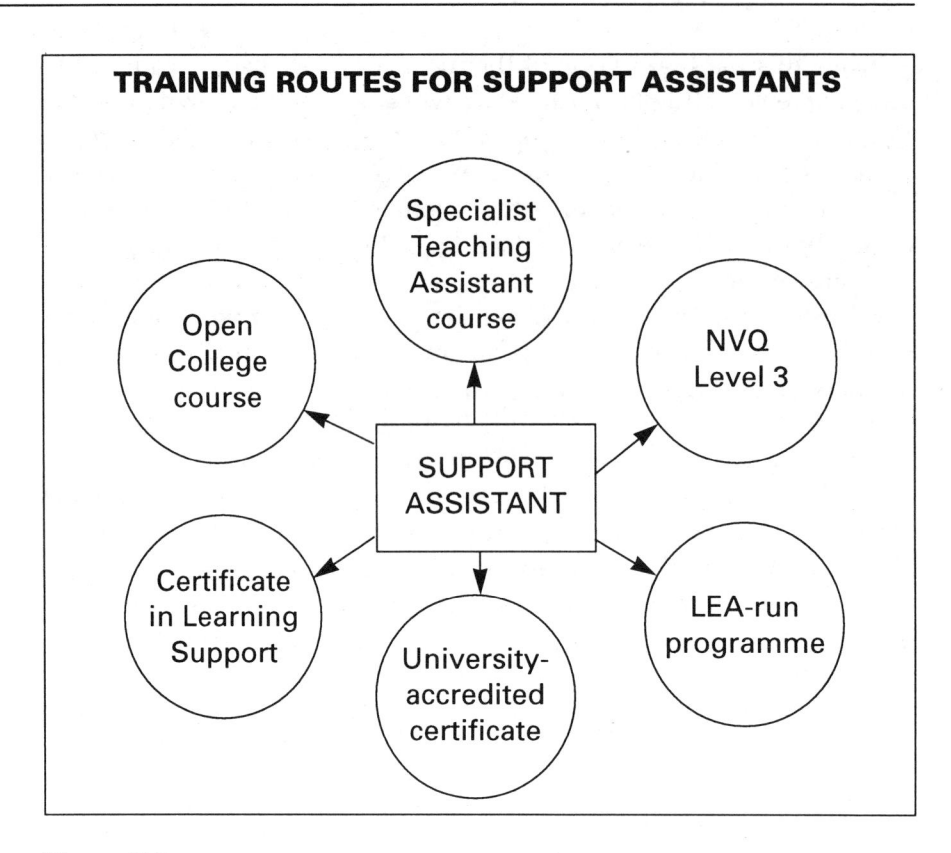

Figure 7.5

Supporting the development of inclusive schools

The publication of the Green Paper *Excellence for All Children* (DfEE 1997a) has encouraged a large number of LEAs to revisit the issue of inclusion and to review their current practices. This, together with a growing pressure from parents, is likely to result in a steady increase in the number of disabled students in the mainstream. While there are some encouraging noises from the Government about 'pump priming' for new initiatives, it is unlikely that much new money will be forthcoming. It is, therefore, essential that schools and LEAs look towards maximising the effectiveness of existing resources.

The traditional approach to integration has been for schools to expect children to adapt and fit into existing systems. Additional resources have then been used to 'paper over the cracks'. In the inclusive school, on the other hand, it is the system that changes to meet the needs of the students. As Sebba and Ainscow (1996) comment, inclusive education is a process that involves the school reconsidering and restructuring its curricular organisation and provision and allocating resources to enhance equality of opportunity for all pupils. Developing inclusive classrooms requires teachers to view their task somewhat differently from previously (Sebba and Sachdev 1997) and as a consequence, to change their practice.

Where in-class support is used, it is vital that some of the dangers noted earlier are avoided. OFSTED (1996) have defined what they consider to be the characteristics of successful in-class support in ordinary schools and these are summarised in Figure 7.6. But to enable this to happen, considerable time and effort will be required in retraining classroom teachers. As one teacher from the Kirklees Inclusive Education Project quoted by Sebba *et al.* (1996) commented:

> We haven't been trained to work with support staff. Teachers need training in how to work with support and the support staff need training in how to work with teachers. We don't need INSET on how to support children but on how to work with another adult. You can't just put bodies in the classroom.

The ability to work collaboratively with others and manage additional adults in the classroom, has now been recognised as a core skill for newly qualified teachers (DfEE 1997b). However, it is vital that a similar programme of training is put in place for experienced staff, if schools are to become progressively more inclusive. Teachers who work in teams, according to Rief and Heimburge (1996):

FEATURES OF HIGH QUALITY IN-CLASS SUPPORT

1. Good team working between support staff and class teacher, i.e. joint planning to allow pupils with SEN to work on the same curriculum area or theme as the rest of the class, but at an appropriate level

2. The support teacher or special support assistant (SSA) being well supplied with information about work to be attempted

3. The support teacher introducing additional materials and strategies to enable pupils with SEN to take part. Often these are of use to a wider group of pupils

4. The support teacher or SSA working, for example, with a more able group, enabling the class teacher to focus on those pupils who need more help

5. Ensuring that pupils of all abilities are adequately challenged to solve problems, reflect, formulate strategies, and act independently, i.e. it is not helpful to the pupils if the support teacher or SSA largely does the work for the child

6. Ensuring the integration of pupils with SEN into the whole class

---

Figure 7.6

- gain a deeper knowledge of their own teaching style;
- acquire a renewed sense of enthusiasm;
- create a healthier, more balanced environment for everyone involved;
- are inspired to stay abreast of current ideas in the field;
- gain an opportunity to extend their interpersonal skills.

To move forward, schools need to become collaborative learning environments with a shared goal. Villa (1998) defines four major blocks to the development of inclusive communities:

1. inadequate teacher preparation,
2. inappropriate organisational structures, policies, practices and procedures,
3. inadequate attention to creating new cultures,
4. leadership that is naive or cowardly.

To develop more inclusive practices, according to Knoster (1991), schools need a vision, skills, incentives, resources and an action plan (see Figure 7.7). Without the vision, there will be confusion as no one will be sure where they are heading. Without the requisite skills, staff will be anxious and unable to implement new strategies. Without incentives, there will be resistance from individuals or groups blocking progress. Without resources, staff committed to change will experience frustration and may lose heart. Finally, without an action plan, those involved will go round and round on a treadmill, achieving little.

```
MANAGING COMPLEX CHANGE

Vision + Skills + Incentives + Resources + Action Plan = Change
         Skills + Incentives + Resources + Action Plan = Confusion
Vision          + Incentives + Resources + Action Plan = Anxiety
Vision + Skills             + Resources + Action Plan = Resistance
Vision + Skills + Incentives            + Action Plan = Frustration
Vision + Skills + Incentives + Resources              = Treadmill
```

Figure 7.7

One school that has gone a long way along the road to inclusion is Langdon School in Newham (Macaulay 1998). Here, students with SEN are fully part of all aspects of school life and are not a bolt-on section of the school. This is ensured by special needs having a high profile within the school; there is full senior management support for SEN issues and the SENCO is a senior teacher on the senior management team.

Clearly there is a shared vision here which is then backed up by staff training. All teaching staff have been included, over a period of time in training which has covered differentiation, partnership teaching and identifying and assessing SEN. Particular attention has been paid to the development of appropriate skills for both newly qualified teachers and LSAs.

The development of communication systems across the school is seen as a key to successful practice. Each teacher within the learning support department is linked to one or more subject departments. Communication is enhanced further by the use of a SEN notice board in the staffroom, announcements at weekly staff briefings, a weekly staff bulletin and policies for support, partnership teaching and differentiation in the staff handbook.

LSAs work in a team under a senior assistant and her deputy. These LSA managers have responsibility for organising rotas and for promoting a team spirit. As Macauley (1998) concludes, 'At Langdon we have watched students . . . who have made social and academic progress beyond what even we had expected'. Further, as the numbers and level of need of students with SEN has increased, there has been no concomitant drop in academic success. Finally she comments: 'It is noteworthy that in the last three years when inclusion has significantly increased at Langdon, there have been no permanent exclusions'.

In this school there is support for students, support for teachers, support for LSAs and support for the SENCO. Together they ensure that the needs of the whole school community are being met. For as Thomas *et al.* (1998) emphasise:

> The education system is at the beginning of a new inclusive adventure and it will take decades to develop practice. But there can be no doubt that a non-segregated diverse population of children and young people in schools will produce schools which are more sensitive and more people orientated . . . . In inclusive schools all will thrive.

References

AFASIC (1996) *Principles for Educational Provision*. London: AFASIC.

Ainscow, M. (1995) 'Education for all: making it happen', *Support for Learning* **10**(4), 147–55.

Allan, J. (1995) 'How are we doing? Teachers views on the effectiveness of co-operative teaching', *Support for Learning* **10**(3), 127–31.

ALSS (1991) *Guidelines for Special Support Assistants*. Assessment and Learning Support Service, Calderdale LEA.

Audit Commission (1992) *Getting the Act Together*. London: HMSO.

Bairstow, P., Cochrane, R., Hur, J. (1993) *Evaluation of Conductive Education for Children with Cerebral Palsy*. London: Department for Education/HMSO.

Balshaw, M. (1991) *Help in the Classroom*. London: David Fulton Publishers.

Balshaw, M. (1998) 'Call for assistants', *Special*, Spring, 11–12.

Bartholomew, L. and Bruce, T. (1993) *Getting to Know You*. London: Hodder & Stoughton.

Baskind, S. and Thompson, D. (1995) 'Using assistants to support the educational needs of pupils with learning difficulties', *Educational and Child Psychology* **12**(2), 46–58.

Bastiani, J. (1989) *Working with Parents: a Whole School Approach*. Windsor: NFER-Nelson.

Bearn, A. and Smith, C. (1998) 'How learning support is perceived by mainstream colleagues', *Support for Learning* **13**(1), 14–20.

Bell, F. (1988) 'Support of mainstreamed children with special educational needs by non-teaching assistants', *Division of Education and Child Psychology Newsletter* **29**, 28–31.

Best, R. (1991) 'Support teaching in a comprehensive school', *Support for Learning* **6**(1), 27–32.

Bibby, G. (1990) 'An evaluation of in-class support in a secondary school', *Support for Learning* **5**(1), 37–42.

Bone, K. and Mason, D. (1994) 'Sink or swim: supporting Down's syndrome children in mainstream schools', *Special Needs*.

Bourne, J. and McPake, J. (1991) *Partnership Teaching*. London: HMSO.

Bruce, T. (1987) *Early Childhood Education.* Sevenoaks: Hodder & Stoughton.

Burridge, P. (1995) 'I've got a reason', *Special Children* **88**, 31–4.

Bury (1996) *The Induction of Special Support Assistants.* Bury MBC.

Cade, L. and Caffyn, R. (1995) 'Family planning for special needs', *Support for Learning* **10**(2), 70–74.

Carpenter, B. and Shoesmith, C. (1992) *The Child with Special Needs – An Information Pack.* Solihull MBC.

Casteel, J. (1985) quoted in Woolf and Bassett (1988) 'How classroom assistants respond', *British Journal of Special Education,* **15**(2), 62–5.

Caswell, J. (1992) *A Model for Special Educational Needs Auxiliaries and Schools Working Together Effectively,* 23–5. Northumberland County Council.

Caswell, J. and Pinner, S. (1996) *SENAT: Special Educational Needs Assistants and Teachers.* Northumberland County Council.

Challen, M. and Majors, K. (1997) *Learning to Support.* Bristol: Lucky Duck.

Cheminais, R. (1997) 'Can I help?', *Special Children* **103,** 15–19.

Clayton, T. *et al.* (1989) *SAINTS: Special Assistants In-Service Training Scheme.* Wiltshire Education Department.

Clayton, T. (1990) 'Induction courses for special welfare assistants', *Educational Psychology in Practice* **6**(2), 44–52.

Clayton, T. (1993) 'Welfare assistants in the classroom – problems and solutions', *Educational Psychology in Practice* **8**(4), 191–7.

Cole, K. *et al.* (1989) 'Comparison of two service delivery models: in-class and out-of-class therapy approaches', *Paediatric Physical Therapist* **1**(2), 4–54.

Coopers and Lybrand (1992) *Within Reach: Access for Disabled Children – Mainstream Education.* London: NUT/Spastics Society.

Copeland, I. (1990) 'Support across the curriculum', *British Journal of Special Education* **17**(1), 9–12.

CRE (1986) *The Teaching of English as a Second Language.* London: Commission for Racial Equality.

Cummins, J. (1984) *Bilingualism and Special Education.* Avon: Multilingual Matters.

Curry, M. and Broomfield, C. (1994) *Personal and Social Education for Primary Schools Through Circle Time.* Stafford: NASEN Publications.

Cyster, R., Clift, P., Battle, S. (1979) *Parental Involvement in Primary Schools.* Slough: NFER.

DES (1967) *Children and their Primary Schools.* (The Plowden Report.) London: HMSO.

DES (1970) *Education (Handicapped Children) Act.* London: HMSO.

DES (1975) *A Language for Life.* (The Bullock Report.) London: HMSO.

DES (1978) *Special Educational Needs.* (The Warnock Report.) London: HMSO.

DES (1981) *Education Act.* London: HMSO.

DES (1986) *Education Act.* London: HMSO.

DES (1990) *Staffing for Pupils with Special Educational Needs.* (Circular 11/90). London: DES.

DES (1991) *Parents and Schools. Aspects of Parental Involvement in Primary and Secondary Schools.* London: HMSO.

DES (1992) *Non-teaching Staff in School: A Review by HMI.* London: HMSO.

De Vault, M., Harnischfeger, A., Wiley, D. (1977) *Curricula, Personnel Resources and Grouping Strategies.* Group for Policy Studies in Education, Central Midwestern Regional Laboratory.

DfE (1994a) *Code of Practice on the Identification and Assessment of Special Educational Needs.* London: Department for Education.

DfE (1994b) *The Organisation of Special Educational Provision.* (Circular 6/94.) London: Department for Education.

DfEE (1997a) *Excellence For All Children: Meeting Special Educational Needs.* London: HMSO.

DfEE (1997b) *Standards for the Award of Qualified Teacher Status.* (Circular 1/97.) London: HMSO.

DoH (1992) *Guidance and Regulations Covering the Children Act 1989.* Volumes 1–10. London: HMSO.

DoH (1993) *Permissible Forms of Control in Children's Residential Care.* Available from the Department of Health, London.

Doyle, M. (1997) *The Paraprofessional's Guide to the Inclusive Classroom.* Baltimore: Paul Brookes Publishing.

Duffield, J. (1998) 'Learning experiences, effective schools and social context', *Support for Learning* **13**(1), 3–9.

Duthie, J. (1970) *Primary School Survey: A Study of the Teacher's Day.* Edinburgh: HMSO.

Dyer, C. (1988) 'Which support?', *Support for Learning* **3**(1), 6–11.

Edwards, C. (1985) 'On launching a support service', *British Journal of Special Education* **12**(2), 53–4.

Fletcher-Campbell, F. (1992) 'How can we use an extra pair of hands?', *British Journal of Special Education* **19**(4), 141–3.

Fox, G. (1993) *A Handbook for Special Needs Assistants.* London: David Fulton Publishers.

Fox, G. (1998) *A Handbook for Learning Support Assistants.* London: David Fulton Publishers.

Fullan, M. (1992) *Successful School Improvements.* Milton Keynes: Open University Press.

Garnett, J. (1988) 'Support teaching: taking a closer look', *British Journal of Special Education* **15**(1), 15–18.

Giangreco, M., York, J., Rainforth, B. (1989) 'Providing related services to learners with severe handicaps in educational settings: pursuing the least restrictive option', *Paediatric Physical Therapist* **1**(2), 55–63.

Gibbons, P. (1991) *Learning to Learn in a Second Language.* Newtown, New South Wales: Primary English Teaching Association.

Goacher, B. et al.(1988) *Provision and Policy for Special Educational Needs.* London: Cassell.

Gold, R. and Szemerenyi, S. (1998) *Running a School: Legal Duties and Responsibilities.* Bristol: Jordan Publishing.

Gravelle, M. (1996) *Supporting Bilingual Learners in Schools.* Stoke-on-Trent: Trentham Books.

Hall, D. (1995) *Assessing the Needs of Bilingual Pupils.* London: David Fulton Publishers.

Hanko, G. (1995) *Special Needs in Ordinary Classrooms.* London: David Fulton Publishers.

Harris, J. and Hewett, D. (1996) *Positive Approaches to Challenging Behaviour.* Kidderminster: First Draft Publications.

Hart, S. (1986) 'In class support teaching: tackling Fish', *British Journal of Special Education* **13**(2), 57–8.

Hart, S. (1991) 'The collaborative dimension: risks and rewards of collaboration', in McLaughlin, C. and Rouse, M. (eds) *Supporting Schools.* London: David Fulton Publishers.

Haykin, W. and Pierce, A. (1989) *A Strategy for Appraisal.* CCDU, The University of Leeds.

Hewett, D. and Arnett, A. (1996) 'Guidance on the use of physical force by staff in educational establishments', *British Journal of Special Education* **23**(3), 130–33.

Hill, S. (1997) 'The relevance and value of music therapy for children with Rett Syndrome', *British Journal of Special Education* **24**(3), 124–9.

Hirstwood, R. (1994) 'Safe and sound', *Special Children* **79**, 34–6.

HMI (1991) *Interdisciplinary Support for Young Children with Special Educational Needs.* London: DES.

Hockley, L. (1985) 'On being a support teacher', *British Journal of Special Education* **12**(1), 27–9.

HSE (1992) *Manual Handling Operations Regulations.* Sheffield: Health and Safety Executive.

Humberside (1995) *Almost 200 Tried and Tested Ideas for Involving Parents in their Child's Education.* Humberside County Council.

Inglese, J. (1996) 'Special teachers? Perceptions of the special expertise required for effective special educational needs teaching and advisory work', *Support For Learning* **11**(2), 83–7.

Ireson, J. (1992) 'Collaboration in support systems', *British Journal of Special Education* **19**(2), 56–8.

Johnston, J. (1984) 'Problems of pre-kindergarten teachers: a basis for reexamining teacher education practices', *Journal of Teacher Education* **35**(2), 33–7.

Jordan, A. (1994) *Skills in Collaborative Classroom Consultation.* London: Routledge.

Kenward, H. (1997) *Integrating Pupils with Disabilities in Mainstream Schools.* London: David Fulton Publishers.

Knoster, T. (1991) Presentation at TASH Conference, Washington, DC.

Kovic, S. (1996) 'Peer coaching to facilitate inclusion. A job embedded staff development model', *Journal of Staff Development* **17**(1), 28–31.

Kozma, I. (1995) 'The basic principles and present practice of conductive education', *European Journal of Special Needs Education* **10**(2), 111–23.

Lacey, P. and Lomas, J. (1993) *Support Services and the Curriculum.* London: David Fulton Publishers.

Lally, M. (1991) *The Nursery Teacher in Action.* London: Paul Chapman Publishing.

Lee, B. and Henkhuzens, Z. (1996) *Integration in Progress*. Slough: NFER.

Le Laurin, K. and Risley, T. (1972) 'The organisation of day care environments: "zone" versus "man to man" staff assignments', *Journal of Applied Behavioural Analysis* **5**(3), 225–32.

Lloyd, C. (1997) 'Inclusive education for children with special educational needs in the early years', in Wolfendale, S. (ed.) *Meeting Special Educational Needs in the Early Years*. London: David Fulton Publishers.

Lloyd-Smith, W. (1995) 'NHS Trusts, the market and occupational therapy', *British Journal of Therapy and Rehabilitation* **2**(9), 473–77.

Lorenz, S. (1992) 'Supporting special needs assistants in mainstream schools', *Educational and Child Psychology* **9**(4), 25–33.

Lorenz, S. (1996) *Supporting Support Assistants*. Manchester: Stephanie Lorenz.

Lorenz, S. (1998a) *Children with Down's Syndrome*. London: David Fulton Publishers.

Lorenz, S. (1998b) *The Support Assistant's Survival Guide*. Manchester: Stephanie Lorenz.

Lovey, J. (1995) *Supporting Special Educational Needs in Secondary School Classrooms*. London: David Fulton Publishers.

Lovey, J. (1996) 'Concepts in identifying effective classroom support', *Support for Learning* **11**(1), 9–12.

Macauley, A. (1998) 'The development and successes of inclusion at Langdon Secondary School', *Network News* **23**, 13–17. Network 81.

Mackey, S. and McQueen, J. (1998) 'Exploring the association between integrated therapy and inclusive education', *British Journal of Special Education* **25**(1), 22–7.

Male, D. (1996a) 'Who goes to MLD schools?', *British Journal of Special Education* **23**(1), 35–41.

Male, D. (1996b) 'Who goes to SLD schools?', *Journal of Applied Research in Intellectual Disabilities* **9**(4), 307–23.

Margerison, A. (1997) 'Class teachers and the role of classroom assistants in the delivery of special educational needs', *Support for Learning* **12**(4), 166–9.

Marland, M. (1978) 'The teacher, the ancillary and inner-city education'. Unpublished paper quoted in Mortimore, P., Mortimore, J., Thomas, H. (eds) (1994) *Managing Associate Staff*. London: Paul Chapman Publishing.

Mason, A. (1978) 'The headteacher's role in the development of staff', in Craig, I. (ed.) *Primary School Management in Action*. Harlow: Longman.

McBrien, J. and Weightman, J. (1980) 'The effect of room management procedures on the engagement of profoundly retarded children', *British Journal of Mental Subnormality* **26**(1), 38–46.

McNamara, S. and Moreton, G. (1993) *Teaching Special Needs: Strategies and Activities for Children in the Primary Classroom*. London: David Fulton Publishers.

McQueen, J. and McLellan, L. (1994) *Access to the Curriculum*. Southampton: University of Southampton Rehabilitation Research Unit.

McQueen, J. and McLellan, L. (1996) *Educational Provision for Pupils with Cerebral Palsy*. Southampton: University of Southampton Rehabilitation Research Unit.

McQuillan, R. (1987) *Parents in the Classroom*. Derby: Professional Association of Teachers.

Miller, C. (1996) 'Sound sense: how to make sense of speech and language difficulties', *Special*, Spring, 20–24.

Mills, R. and Mills, J. (1993) *Bilingualism in the Primary School*. London: Routledge.

Mittler, P. (1993) *Teacher Education for Special Educational Needs*. Stafford: NASEN Publications.

Morris, N. and Parker, P. (1997) 'Reviewing the teaching and learning of children with special educational needs: enabling whole school responsibility', *British Journal of Special Education* **24**(4), 163–7.

Mortimore, J. and Mortimore, P. (1984) 'Parents and school', *Education* **164**(14), i–iv.

Mortimore, P., Mortimore, J. and Thomas, H. (eds) (1994) *Managing Associate Staff*. London: Paul Chapman Publishing.

Moyles, J. (1997) *Jills of All Trades*. London: ATL Publications.

NCC (1993) *Special Needs and the National Curriculum: Opportunity and Challenge*. York: National Curriculum Council.

Newman, K. and Rose, R. (1990) 'Self evaluation at Wren Spinney', *British Journal of Special Education* **17**(1), 12–14.

Nias, J., Southworth, G., Yeomans, R. (1989) *Staff Relationships in the Primary School*. London: Cassell Educational.

Nolan, A. and Gersch, I. (1996) 'More than an extra pair of hands', *Special Children* **91**, 10–15.

OFSTED (1994) *Educational Support for Minority Ethnic Communities*. London: HMSO.

OFSTED (1996) *Promoting High Achievement*. London: HMSO.

O'Grady, C. (1990) *Integration Working*. Bristol: Centre for Studies of Inclusive Education.

OPTIS (1988) *Working Together*. Oxfordshire County Council.

OPTIS (1992) *Helping in School*. Bedfordshire County Council.

Pardoe, J. and Attfield, R. (1989) 'Appraisal: the Salford experience', *British Journal of Special Education* **16**(3), 103–5.

Peter, M. (1993) 'All in a day's work', *Special*, June, 37–8.

Pickup, M. (1995) 'The role of the special educational needs co-ordinator: developing philosophy and practice', *Support for Learning* **10**(2), 88–92.

Pothecary, P. and McCarthy, D. (1996) *Special Support Assistants: A Manual for Schools*. Ilford: Specialist Matters.

Quah, M. and Jones, K. (1997) 'Reshaping learning support in a rapidly developing society', *Support for Learning* **12**(1), 38–42.

Rees, M. (1995) 'Support in the early years classroom', *Early Years* **16**(1), 41–5.

Rief, S. and Heimburge, J. (1996) *How to Reach and Teach all Students in the Inclusive Classroom*. London: Prentice-Hall International.

RNIB (1994) *Including Visually Impaired Pupils*. London: RNIB Education.
Russell, P. (1997) 'Don't forget us', *British Journal of Special Education* **24**(2), 60–65.
SCAA (1996) *Planning the Curriculum: for Pupils with Profound and Multiple Learning Difficulties*. Hayes: SCAA Publications.
Sebba, J. (1992) 'A National Curriculum for all', *Special*, September, 19–21.
Sebba, J. and Ainscow, M. (1996) 'International developments in inclusive education – mapping the issues', *Cambridge Journal of Education* **26**, 5–19.
Sebba, J. and Sachdev, D. (1997) *What Works in Inclusive Education?* Barkingside: Barnados.
Sebba, J., Ainscow, M., Lakin, S. (1996) *Developing Inclusive Education at Rawthorpe High School*. Barkingside: Barnados.
Shaw, L. (1997) *Inclusion in Action*. Bristol: Centre for Studies in Inclusive Education.
Skaalvik, E. (1990) 'Attributions of perceived academic results and relations with self esteem in senior high schools', *Scandinavian Journal of Educational Research* **34**(4), 27–34.
Sloper, T. and Tyler, S. (1992) 'Integration of children with severe learning difficulties in mainstream schools', *Education and Child Psychology* **9**(4), 34–45.
Smith, C. (1982) 'Helping colleagues cope: a consultant role for the remedial teacher', *Remedial Education* **17**(2), 75–9.
Starr, A. and Lacey, P. (1996) 'Multidisciplinary assessment: a case study', *British Journal of Special Education* **23**(2), 57–61.
Stevens, L. and Roulstone, S. (1991) 'Speech therapists and teachers working together', *Educational and Child Psychology* **8**(3), 84–92.
Swafford, J. (1998) 'Teachers supporting teachers through peer coaching', *Support for Learning* **13**(2), 54–8.
Sydney, A. (1993) 'Pharaohs and candyfloss', *Special Children* **66**, 19–20.
Taylor, G., Dobson, S., Staves, L. (1993) 'Collaborative working practices in special schools', *Down's Syndrome: Research and Practice* **1**(2), 84–6.
Thomas, G. (1990) 'Evaluating support', *Support for Learning* **5**(1), 30–36.
Thomas, G. (1992) *Effective Classroom Teamwork*. London: Routledge.
Thomas, G. and Jackson, B. (1986) 'The whole-school approach to integration', *British Journal of Special Education* **13**(1), 27–9.
Thomas, G., Walker, D., Webb, J. (1998) *The Making of the Inclusive School*. London: Routledge.
Tizard, J., Schofield, W., Hewison, J. (1982) 'Collaboration between teachers and parents in assisting children's reading', *British Journal of Educational Psychology* **52**, 1–15.
Turner, P. (1985) 'Headship. Aspects of the role', in Bowers, T. (ed.) *Management and the Special School*. London: Croom Helm.

Villa, R. (1998) *How to Solve the Inclusion Puzzle in Under 8 Hours.* Lecture Guide. Colchester: Bayridge Consortium.

Vincent, C. et al. (1995) 'Policy and practice: the changing nature of special educational provision in schools', *British Journal of Special Education* **22**(1), 4–11.

Wade, B. and Moore, M. (1993) *Experiencing Special Education.* Buckingham: Open University Press.

Ware, J. and Evans, P. (1987) 'Room management is not enough', *British Journal of Special Education* **14**(2), 78–80.

Watmough, M. (1986) *Staff Appraisal in a School Psychological Service.* Cumbria Psychological Service.

Welding, J. (1996) 'In-class support: a successful way of meeting individual students' needs', *Support for Learning* **11**(3), 113–17.

Wheal, R. (1995) 'Unleashing individual potential: a team approach', *Support for Learning* **10**(2), 83–7.

Williamson, J. (1989) 'An extra radiator? Teachers' views of support teaching and withdrawal in developing the English of bilingual pupils', *Educational Studies* **15**(3), 315–26.

Wilson, D. and Newton, C. (1996) 'A Circle of Friends', *Special Children* **89**, 7–9.

Wolfendale, S. (1992) *Empowering Parents and Teachers.* London: Cassell.

Woods, P. and Cullen, C. (1983) 'Determinants of staff behaviour in long term care', *Behavioural Psychotherapy* **11**, 4–17.

Woolf, M. and Bassett, S. (1988) 'How classroom assistants respond', *British Journal of Special Education* **15**(2), 62–5.

Wright, J. (1996) 'Teachers and therapists, the evolution of a partnership', *Child Language, Teaching and Therapy* **12**(1), 13–16.

Wright, J. and Graham, J. (1997) 'Where and when do speech and language therapists work with teachers?', *British Journal of Special Education* **24**(4), 171–4.

Index

Abuse 22, 85.
Appraisal 53, 74, 86–89.

Behaviour management 21–23, 40, 47, 49, 60.
Bilingual assistants 7, 30–33, 49.

CLASS 9, 87.
Classroom assistants 2, 27–30, 66–68.
Code of Practice 7, 17, 28, 45, 61.
Counselling 21, 40, 48, 59, 87.

Early years 25–7, 60.
EBD 21–23, 60.

Funding 7–9, 45, 65.

Health & safety 81–86.
Hearing impairment 7, 14, 59.

IEPs 3, 15, 19, 79.
Inclusive education 3, 29, 31, 44, 60, 92–95.
Independence 13, 19, 29, 39, 46, 59, 81.
Induction 35, 45, 75, 77–80.
Insurance cover 81–85.

Job descriptions 10, 20, 27, 50, 54–55, 68–74, 79, 85.

Learning difficulties 13–14, 60.
Lifting and handling 81–84.

Management issues 9, 28, 69, 77, 86–7, 90–91, 94.
Medication 18, 85.
Models of support 4–6, 17–19, 39–40, 49.
Mother tongue teaching 14, 31–33.

Multidisciplinary teams 10, 57–61.

National Curriculum 1, 13, 26, 56, 59, 61.
Nursery nurses 1, 8, 25–27.

Observation skills 19, 21–22, 40–41, 57, 61.
Occupational therapy 18, 59.

Parental involvement 2, 10, 33–37, 59, 68, 81.
Partnership teaching 42–45, 49, 95.
Peer support 16, 19, 31, 44–45.
Physical disability 2, 17–20, 81.
Physiotherapy 18, 57–59.
Planning 5, 13, 31, 42, 44, 46, 61, 75–7.
Primary schools 25–37.

Qualifications 7, 25, 66, 91.

Record keeping 5, 21, 31, 44, 85.
Recruitment 8–9, 65–68.
Restraint 85–86.
Roles and responsibilities 3, 10, 26–29, 41, 44, 54, 62–64, 68.
Room management 61–64.

Secondary schools 4–5, 7, 39–52.
Self esteem 5, 16, 21, 39.
SENCOs 9, 39, 47–49, 68, 79, 86–88.
Special schools 2, 6–7, 10, 53–64.
SpLD 15–17.
Speech therapy 18, 57–61.
Staff development 37, 50, 75–6, 94.
Support assistants 9–10, 45–48, 53–56, 68.
Support departments 4, 39, 77, 95.
Support groups 9, 53, 74, 87.
Support services 4, 7, 39, 65.
Support teachers 4, 7, 10, 22, 39–42.

Teamwork 6, 23–25, 42–44, 57–59, 74–77, 88, 93.
Training 9–10, 53–54, 56, 77–80, 85–86, 90–94.

Visual impairment 7, 49, 59.

Whole school responses 21, 41, 43, 74–77, 81, 91, 94–95.
Withdrawal 2, 5, 13, 56–57.